Finding the Faith
Devotions for
Youth Ministry

Group

Loveland, Colorado

Group's R.E.A.L. Guarantee to you:

Every Group resource incorporates our R.E.A.L. approach to ministry—
a unique philosophy that results in long-term retention and life
transformation. It's ministry that's:

**This is EARL.
He's R.E.A.L.
mixed up.
(Get it?)**

Relational
Because student-to-
student interaction
enhances learning and
builds Christian
friendships.

Experiential
Because what students
experience sticks with
them up to 9 times
longer than what they
simply hear or read.

Applicable
Because the aim of
Christian education is
to be both hearers and
doers of the Word.

Learner-based
Because students learn
more and retain it
longer when the
process is designed
according to how they
learn best.

Finding the Faith Devotions for Youth Ministry
Copyright © 2002 Group Publishing, Inc.

Visit our Web site: **www.grouppublishing.com**

Credits
Contributing Authors: Tim Baker, Jennifer L. Easley, Debbie Gowensmith, Bristow Hood, Jan Kershner, Kelly Martin, Erin McKay, Julie Meiklejohn, Kristi Rector, Christina Schofield, and Katherine S. Zimmerman
Editors: Amy Simpson and Kelli B. Trujillo
Creative Development Editor: Jim Kochenburger
Chief Creative Officer: Joani Schultz
Copy Editor: Deirdre Brouer
Art Director: Kari K. Monson
Computer Graphic Artist: Joyce Douglas
Cover Art Director: Jeff A. Storm
Cover Design: Blukazoo Studios
Illustrator: Michael Morris
Production Manager: Dodie Tipton

Library of Congress Cataloging-in-Publication Data
Finding the faith devotions for youth ministry
    p. cm.
  Includes index.
  ISBN 0-7644-2200-6 (alk. paper)
    1. Church group work with teenagers. 2. Christian education of teenagers. 3. Christian teenagers--Prayer-books and devotions--English. I. Group Publishing.
BV4447 .F56 2001
268'.433--dc21

                                                2001033471

10 9 8 7 6 5 4 3 2 1   11 10 09 08 07 06 05 04 03 02

Printed in the United States of America.

Contents

Introduction

I f your youth ministry is like most, your teenagers are an eclectic mix. Besides a variety of ages, social groups, and family backgrounds, your students reflect a wide range of spiritual experiences. Some probably have been involved in church all their lives. Others have only recently begun to explore what Christianity is all about.

Regardless of the differences, it's possible that none of your teenagers have a truly solid foundation of understanding in key Christian issues. Even those who have grown up in Sunday school may not understand why Jesus' resurrection is important or who angels really are.

Use these devotions to help your teenagers explore some of the key issues of the Christian faith. *Finding the Faith Devotions for Youth Ministry* covers basic topics such as God's love, sin and forgiveness, heaven and hell, the church, sharing faith, salvation, creation, worship, and more.

These twenty- to thirty-minute devotions present Christian teachings in a low-key, nonthreatening way your students will appreciate, especially those who are unfamiliar with Christianity. At the same time, the devotions are fun and challenging for teenagers who have a more seasoned faith.

Use the devotions in this book to help your students understand basic truths of Christianity. You'll be helping to build in them a solid foundation of faith.

Getting to Know God

Topic: God

Supplies: You'll need paper, pens or pencils, and Bibles.

Devotion

Begin by telling the group about someone you're close to, whom the group doesn't know well, such as a good friend, a sibling, or a parent. Describe that person's character, especially what makes that person special to you. For example, you could say, "I'd like you all to know my sister better. She's one of those people who's always smiling and cracking jokes. She always sees the positive side of things." You could even include a true story that highlights the person's character—something that will help your students get to know that person better.

After you've described someone, encourage the students to ask you questions that will help them know that person even better. After answering a few questions, ask:

• **How do you get to know someone?**

• **What does the way we describe someone communicate about how we feel about that person?**

Say: **It takes time to get to know someone, doesn't it? After we've spent time with people, we get an idea of who they are and what they are like based on what they say and do. We start assigning adjectives such as "funny" or "trusting" to them, and that's how we describe them to others. Our descriptions reveal how we feel about them.**

Have students form pairs, and challenge students to practice getting to know each other. Distribute paper and pens or pencils, and tell students they'll be helping the rest of the group get to know their partners better in a few minutes. Say: **You can choose how you'll introduce and describe your partner to the rest of the group. You can introduce your partner as a guest on a game show, interview your partner as part of a talk show, write a** book-cover biography, or write a newspaper personal ad. Just be sure your description helps others get to know your partner's character.

After about five minutes, have partners take turns introducing each other. If you have a large group, you may want pairs to form groups of four or six and introduce their partners to just those group members.

Afterward, ask:

• **What other methods do you use to get to know others better?**

• **How do you get to know God better?**

• **What similarities are there between getting to know people better and getting to know God better?**

Say: **Though we may not realize it, we can often get to know God in the same ways we get to know people. By spending time with God, paying attention to what he says and does, and discovering what he's done in the past, we get to know God's character. We have access to a lot of information about God in his Word. In fact, God gave us the Bible so we'd be able to get to know him better. Let's look at an example.**

Have students look up Psalm 33, and ask several volunteers to take turns reading the chapter aloud. Ask half of the students to write down the adjectives that the psalmist uses to describe God, and ask the other half to write down what the psalmist says that God does or has done.

Have students form pairs that include one student who wrote down adjectives and one student who wrote down actions.

Have pairs share their lists with each other and then discuss these questions.

Ask:

• **What do the adjectives in this psalm tell you about God?**

• **What do the actions described in this psalm tell you about God?**

• **How would you feel toward a friend who is right and true and faithful?**

• **How would you feel toward a friend who loves? who helps? who stands firm forever?**

• **What does this psalm lead you to think about God?**

Have pairs use their lists of adjectives and actions to create introductions for God, just as they created introductions for their partners earlier. For example, if a student wrote a personal ad to introduce someone earlier in the activity, that student should write a personal ad to introduce God. Remind students that their introductions should help others better know God's character.

Give pairs about five minutes to work on their introductions for God. Then have each student share his or her introduction with the rest of the group. If you have a lot of students, you may want to have pairs form groups of four or six and share their introductions just within their small groups.

After everyone has presented an introduction, have pairs discuss these questions.

Ask:

- **What is one special thing you learned about God today?**

- **How will you continue to get to know God better?**

Have each person choose a verse about God from Psalm 33 that he or she especially appreciates, and ask partners to read those verses aloud to each other. Then close in prayer, giving students some time to reflect silently on God's character as described in Psalm 33.

2002 (Summer)

How Big Is God?

Topic: God

Supplies: You'll need several small containers; sand; small items such as candy, pennies, golf tees, and paper clips; pens or pencils; sticky notes; paper; Bibles; a bucket; a spoon; and a glass of water.

Devotion

Before the devotion, fill one container with sand. Fill the remaining containers with other small items, with a different item in each container. For example, you may fill one container with pennies, another with candy, and another with golf tees.

As you fill the containers, keep track of the number of items you place in each one. Then write that number on a ~~sticky note, and stick it to the bottom of the container.~~ *seperate pcs of paper* For example, if you place 245 pieces of candy in a container, write "245" on a sticky note, and stick it to the bottom of the container holding the candy. Place whatever number you want on the bottom of the container of sand.

In your meeting area, set up one station for each container. At each station, place a container filled with a different item. Place the container of sand at the last station.

Give each person a piece of paper and a pen or pencil. Say: **Go to each station, and guess how many items have been placed in the container at that station. Write down your guess on your piece of paper.**

When everyone has had a chance to guess how many items are in each container, ask participants to sit together in the middle of the room.

Ask:

• How close do you think you came to guessing the correct number of items in the containers?

• Why was it difficult to guess the number of items in each container?

• Which item made guessing the most difficult? Why?

Go to each station and tell the group what the actual number of items is for each container. Then ask:

• **How close did you actually come to guessing the correct number of items in the containers?**

• **How many of you think I actually counted all the items in the containers?**

Hold up the container of sand and ask:

• **How many of you think I know exactly how many grains of sand are in this container?**

• **Who could possibly know how many grains of sand are in this container?**

Say: **Only God knows exactly how many grains of sand are here. God also knows how many grains of sand are in the entire world!**

Read Isaiah 40:12-31 aloud.

Ask:

• **How big is God?**

Ask a volunteer to read verse 15 again. Place the empty bucket on the floor in front of the teenagers. Dip the spoon in the glass of water, and let the water drip into the bucket. Say: **These drops are like the nations. How tiny and insignificant they are when compared to God.**

Ask:

• **How big is God?**

Say: **Long ago when this psalm was written, people viewed the earth as flat, not round. And yet in verse 22, the Bible says that God "sits enthroned above the circle of the earth."**

Read verse 26 aloud. Say: **It's actually possible to buy and name a star. They're still discovering stars today! And yet this verse says God has already named every star, even the ones we haven't found yet! So I ask you again: How big is God?**

Ask:

• **How do you feel when you think about how big God is?**

- **What does all this mean to you? How does the "bigness" of God affect you personally?**

Say: **It's amazing to think that God is so big; he knows the number of grains of sand on all the beaches. He knows the names of all the stars. God also knows every intimate detail about each and every one of us, and he still loves us.**

My Best Friend

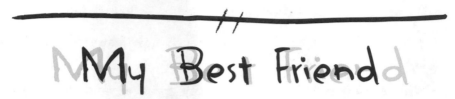

Topic: Jesus

Supplies: You'll need one leather shoelace for every two people, paper, a marker, masking tape, Bibles, scissors, and alphabet beads that spell the word "friend" (one set per person).

Devotion

Before the devotion, tie all the leather shoelaces together, creating a knot at one end and letting the laces dangle at the other end to create a whip. Create two paper signs. One should say, "Roman soldier," and the other should say, "Jesus." Enlist two adult volunteers from the church. Assign one adult the part of the Roman soldier and the other the part of Jesus. Tape the appropriate signs to the actors' clothing. Give the Roman soldier the leather whip, and tell your actors that they'll be acting out the beating Jesus received before he was crucified. Ask them to be seated in the room as youth arrive.

When everyone has arrived, ask:

- **What do you think of when I say the word "friend"?**

- **Who do you consider to be your best friend?**

- **What makes that person your best friend?**

- **Do you think your best friend would gladly lay down his or her life to save yours? Would you do that for your best friend?**

Say: **Jesus said there is no greater love than giving your life for**

another person. Let's take a look at how Jesus viewed friendship.

At this point, have your actors come forward. Have them silently and slowly act out the beating of Jesus. As they're acting, read John 15:13-15 aloud. When you've finished, thank and excuse the actors, but have them leave the whip at the front of the room.

Ask:

• **Why is it significant that Jesus called his followers friends?**

• **How does it feel to know that Jesus loves us enough to call us his friends?**

Read John 15:13-15 again. Say: **Think about the drama we just watched.**

Ask:

• **How did it make you feel?**

• **How do you feel, knowing that Jesus loved you enough not only to call you a friend but also to lay down his pure and sinless life for you?**

• **How would you describe being friends with Jesus?**

• **How have you experienced Jesus' friendship?**

Pass around the leather whip and a pair of scissors. Ask each of the students to cut a piece of the whip that will go around his or her wrist at least one and a half times. When everyone has a piece of leather, say: **We're going to use these pieces of the whip to make friendship bracelets to remind us of Jesus' friendship.**

Give each person a set of alphabet beads that spell the word "friend." Instruct students to make friendship bracelets with the beads by stringing the beads on their pieces of leather. Then have them help each other tie the bracelets around their wrists.

Ask:

• **Why is it significant that we used the leather from the whip to make our bracelets?**

• **How can these bracelets remind us that Jesus is our friend?**

• **How can friendship with Jesus transform our lives?**

Say: **Let your bracelet serve as a reminder that even though we all had a part in Jesus' crucifixion, he still loves all of us enough to call us his friends.**

Jesus to the Rescue

Topic: Jesus

Supplies: You'll need a clear outdoor area, a tape measure or yardstick, five to ten pounds of soil, a candle in a candleholder, water in a watering can, a towel, and Bibles.

Devotion

After enlisting several students to help you carry the supplies, have everyone follow you outside to a parking lot, sidewalk, or grassy area. Measure a lane about five feet wide and sixteen feet long, and have students line up on both sides of the lane. Ask several recruits to help you sprinkle the soil over half the lane (the first eight feet) and then return to the sidelines. Place the candle at the sixteen-foot mark.

Direct participants to the starting line and say: **I want you all to imagine that this candle represents an altar in a church where your fiancé is waiting for your wedding to begin! You are both wearing white from head to toe, and between you and your fiancé stretches a spotless, white aisle runner. The church is packed with people anxiously waiting for you to arrive. But there's a problem. A road crew has just resurfaced the parking lot**.

At this point, use some of the water in the watering can to soak the soil that's been thrown on the ground. Say: **I want you all to imagine that this wet soil is actually tar and I'm the only person who can help you get to the altar.**

Ask:

• **What are your options for arriving at the altar as clean as possible?**

After discussion, ask students to use one of those strategies to cross the newly tarred parking lot. Before they reach the altar, use the remaining water from the watering can and the towel to rinse off and dry students' feet or shoes if necessary. Then have teenagers walk down the aisle to the candle.

Ask:

• **What happened to you on the way to the altar?**

• **How would you feel if your fiancé arrived at your wedding looking dirty or sloppy?**

• **What happened to me in the process of getting you clean before you reached the altar?**

Ask a volunteer to read aloud 2 Corinthians 5:21. Say: **God wants to have a close relationship with us. But he knows we can't get through life without making mistakes and getting dirty along the way. Although he loves us, he can't "marry" himself to us if we are spiritually unclean.**

Ask:

• **Why does our spiritual cleanliness matter to God?**

• **In this demonstration, how was I like Jesus?**

15

• **Why is Jesus willing to help us reach God even if he has to get dirty in the process?**

Say: **Jesus came to help us understand God and to show us how to please God. He came to do away with anything that separates us from God. He came to make us spiritually clean and acceptable to God. Jesus came to our rescue.**

The Holy What?

Topic: Holy Spirit

Supplies: You'll need rubber bands or hair ties, matches, one trick birthday candle (candles that relight after they're blown out) for each student plus one trick birthday candle for every five to six students (trick birthday candles are available in most stores where birthday supplies are sold), modeling clay, masking tape, a cup of water, a cake for the class, copies of "The Holy What?" handout (p. 18), Bibles, and pens or pencils.

Devotion

Before the devotion, place a trick candle in a ball of modeling clay for every five to six students. Place the candles on a table. Tape a line on the floor about eighteen inches away from the table. Be sure to set up this game away from any flammable objects.

Begin by forming teams of five to six students and, to ensure safety, have students with long hair tie their hair back. Emphasize the rule that students must remain kneeling behind the taped line. Have an adult light the candles.

Say: **When I clap my hands, your team may begin taking turns trying to blow the candle out. You may not touch the candle with anything in any way. This means no pinching the candle and definitely no spitting! You may not move beyond the tape mark.**

Clap your hands to begin the game. Students will take turns attempting to

blow out the candles—some may succeed, others will not. When the game is over, be sure to place all candles in the cup of water.

Ask:

- **What was the hardest thing about this activity?**

- **What surprised you? Why?**

Say: **I've often wondered what makes these candles light up again. What do you think makes them relight?**

- **How is faith like these candles?**

Say: **Things happen in life that seem to douse the flames of our faith. Sometimes it feels as if our faith is gone, but then there is a spark, and our faith comes back just as strong or even stronger than before.**

Ask:

- **Have you ever had an experience when it felt as if your faith was doused? What happened?**

- **What are things that challenge your faith?**

- **What do you think keeps faith burning inside of us?**

- **What role does the Holy Spirit play in keeping our faith alive during challenging times?**

The Holy What?

Instructions: Photocopy this page, and cut the copies along the dotted lines. Give a copy of the top half to one pair from each group and a copy of the bottom half to the other pair in each group.

- ✂

The Holy What?

Read the following verses, and discuss the questions with your partner.

Genesis 1:1-5

• Where was the Holy Spirit in the beginning? What did the Holy Spirit do?

Exodus 31:1-5

• When the Spirit of God filled Bezalel, what was he able to do?

1 Corinthians 12:7-11

• Who receives spiritual gifts? Who gives them and how?

- ✂

The Holy What?

Read the following verses, and discuss the questions with your partner.

Psalm 139:7-10

• Where does the Holy Spirit hang out?

John 14:26

• How does the Holy Spirit work to build faith within believers?

Galatians 5:22-23

• How can you tell when the Holy Spirit is working in your life?

- ✂

Read John 14:25-26 aloud. Then say: **When our faith falters, the Holy Spirit reminds us of the truth—the Holy Spirit reminds us of Jesus' love.**

Have students form groups of four and discuss the following questions. Ask:

• **What is the most unusual or the best gift you have ever received?**

• **What did you do with that gift? Where is it now?**

Read Acts 2:38-39 aloud. Then say: **The gift of the Holy Spirit is a pretty awesome gift—but what exactly is this gift? What can the Holy Spirit do for you? We are going to see what we can discover about the Holy Spirit.**

Have students in each group form pairs. Distribute "The Holy What?" handouts to pairs, making sure that one pair from each group gets the top portion of the handout and the other pair receives the bottom portion of the handout. Give students five to ten minutes to explore the verses and answer the questions. When they've finished, have pairs discuss with their original groups what they discovered in their verses.

Bring all of the groups back together, and ask:

• **What are some things you learned about the Holy Spirit and where he is?**

• **What does the Holy Spirit do?**

• **How can knowing the Holy Spirit help you in your Christian walk?**

Give each student a candle and say: **We are going to take turns putting candles on this cake. As you place your candle, think of one way you would like the Holy Spirit to help you in your daily Christian walk. You may share your answer with the group or keep it between you and the Holy Spirit.**

Place your candle on the cake first, and tell the students one area in your life in which you'd like the Holy Spirit to help you grow. Have students do the same. After everyone has placed a candle on the cake, light the candles.

If you have fewer than ten students, you may want to do this activity in a darkened room and have the students light their candles as they place them on the cake.

After the candles are lit, say: **God gives the Holy Spirit as a gift to all Christians. When we believe in Jesus, we each have a new kind of spiritual birthday with an extra-special birthday gift that stays with us forever!**

Pray: **Thank you, God, for the gift of the Holy Spirit in our lives. May the Holy Spirit always help keep the flame of faith burning within all of us as we walk each day with you. In Jesus' name, amen.**

Invite students to help blow out the candles. Cut the cake, and let students enjoy!

Spirit Power

Topic: Holy Spirit

Supplies: You'll need copies of the "Spirit Power" handout (p. 22), a variety of raw vegetables, a dull butter knife, a cutting board, a food processor, Bibles, pens or pencils, and a few trays of fresh vegetables and dip for the students to eat (optional).

Devotion

Say: **I think I'd like to have a salad. Will someone help me make it?**

Have a volunteer begin to chop the vegetables, using the dull butter knife and the cutting board. As the volunteer is chopping the vegetables, say: **You know, I'm getting really hungry! This is just taking too long!**

Pull out the food processor, and show another volunteer how to chop vegetables using the food processor. Ask him or her to finish making the salad. When the vegetables are chopped, thank the volunteers and ask:

• **What made the difference in the two ways of chopping vegetables?**

Invite the students to come up and take some of the fresh vegetables to snack on during the rest of the devotion. You may want to have a few trays of vegetables and dip as well.

Say: **It was much easier and more effective to chop the vegetables using power—the power of electricity. Now let's read about another kind of power.** Have a volunteer read Acts 4:1-13 aloud.

Ask:

• **How did the power of the Holy Spirit affect the people in this passage?**

Say: **The Holy Spirit is one way God shows himself. One of the Holy Spirit's jobs is to give God's followers power to do what he's called them to do.**

Ask:

• **What are some jobs God's followers might do in the world?**

• **How could the Holy Spirit empower God's followers to do those jobs?**

Give each student a "Spirit Power" handout (p. 22) and a pen or pencil. Say: **I'd like you to think about specific ways and specific situations in which you could use the Holy Spirit's power in each of the categories on this handout. Jot down some notes under each category.**

Give students time to do this, and then say: **Now I'd like you to choose the category in which you feel you most need the Holy Spirit's help right now. Form a group with others who chose that category.** Give students a few moments to form their groups.

When teenagers are in groups, say: **Now I'd like you to share with the others in your group the situation you're facing and how you need the Holy Spirit's power. In a moment, you'll be praying for the Holy Spirit's power to rest on each other.** Give groups time to share, and then ask them to pray the prayer on the bottom of the "Spirit Power" handout together.

Say: **Throughout this next week and on an ongoing basis, let's continue to pray for each other. And remember to follow up with others to discover how the Holy Spirit is working in our lives.**

21

Spirit Power

School

Home

Church/Spiritual Life

God, thank you so much for the gift of your Holy Spirit. We ask that you use the power of your Holy Spirit in the situations we're facing. Please help us in the coming week to focus on the Holy Spirit's power in all areas of our lives. In Jesus' name, amen.

Can This Be Destroyed?

Topic: God's Love

Supplies: You'll need poster board; a marker; a tarp (optional); Bibles; a timer or stopwatch; and a variety of used or inexpensive items that students can attempt to destroy, such as an old T-shirt, aluminum foil, a ball of modeling clay, an unwanted CD, paper clips, a sturdy piece of rope, and an inflated balloon. Be sure that some of your destructible items are easy to destroy and that others are difficult to destroy.

Devotion

Before this devotion, write, "Can This Be Destroyed?" across the top of a poster board. Underneath this question, create a chart with these three categories: "Impossible to Destroy," "Difficult to Destroy," and "Easy to Destroy." Because this devotion could get messy, you may want to have it outside or lay down a tarp in your meeting area.

Have teenagers form groups of four or five. Give each group an object to destroy. Show teenagers the "Can This Be Destroyed?" chart. Say: **In your group, you'll have five minutes to destroy the object I've given you. But before you begin, I'd like you to predict how easy or difficult you think it will be to destroy your object. Each of you should come forward and write the name of your object in the appropriate category on this chart.**

When everyone has made a prediction, set a timer or stopwatch for five minutes. Tell groups to begin destroying their objects. When time is up, have groups share their results.

Then ask:

- **What was it like to destroy your object?**

- **Which item was the most difficult to destroy?**

- **What are some other objects that are extremely durable?**

Read Romans 8:35-39 aloud.

Say: **God's love for us is indestructible. It's durable enough to withstand whatever comes our way.**

Ask:

• **How is God's love for you different from a friend's love for you?**

• **How is God's love for you different from a parent's love for you?**

• **How is your love for God different from God's love for you?**

On the backside of the poster board, create two columns with these headings: "Easy to Love" and "Hard to Love." Say: **Let's create a list of qualities that make people easy or hard to love.** As students call out suggestions, write the qualities in the appropriate columns on the poster.

Then ask:

• **Can you share a time you have been difficult for someone to love? How about a time you received a lot of praise or a time you were easy to love?**

Say: **God has loved us at our best and worst, regardless of our failures or successes.**

• **How does unconditional, indestructible love provide a sense of freedom?**

• **What is God's love for us like?**

• **In what ways does God express this love for us?**

• **What do you plan to do in response to God's love?**

Close in prayer, thanking God for his undying love for us.

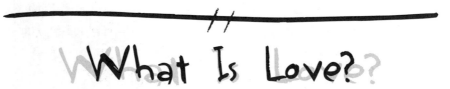

What Is Love?

Topic: God's Love

Supplies: You'll need newsprint, a marker, tape, scissors, red construction paper, pens or pencils, dictionaries, and Bibles.

Devotion

Before this devotion, draw the outline of a giant heart on a sheet of newsprint. Post the newsprint on a wall in your meeting area.

Have teenagers form small groups of two or three, and give each group scissors, pens or pencils, tape, and a supply of red construction paper.

Say: **Today we're going to talk about love. In your group, think of as many words as you can to define love. Cut a heart out of the construction paper, and write each word you think of on the heart.**

Give teenagers up to ten minutes to cut out and write on their red hearts. Circulate among the teenagers, offering help as needed. If they have trouble getting started, tell them to finish the sentence "Love is..." Encourage teenagers to think of all kinds of love, such as love between parent and child, husband and wife, or brother and sister.

After groups have finished, let them take turns taping their red hearts inside the newsprint heart. It's OK if the red hearts "overflow" on the newsprint heart; in fact, that's good! When teenagers have taped all their hearts to the newsprint, give each group a dictionary.

Say: **You've come up with lots of words to describe love. But just to be sure, let's see if there are any definitions you've missed. Look**

up the word "love" in your dictionary, and see if there are any other words to define love. If so, each group may add one more red heart to the newsprint.

After groups have added more definitions, ask:

• **Are you satisfied with the way you've defined love? Explain.**

• **Is there anything you'd like to add to this definition? If so, what?**

Say: **I think we should check one more source to make sure our definition is complete.** Give each group a Bible, and have a volunteer in each group read aloud 1 Corinthians 13:4-8a. Say: **In your group, think of a one-word definition of love that summarizes each phrase of this verse. The first two phrases are easy: love is "patient" and love is "kind." For some of the other phrases, you'll have to turn the phrase around to come up with a one-word definition. For example, the next phrase, "It does not envy," could be summarized in the word "satisfied." I'll give you a few minutes to go through the phrases. Write each new word you come up with on a new red heart.**

Give teenagers several minutes to read the Bible passage and make new hearts. Then invite teenagers to explain what they've written and to add their new hearts to the newsprint.

Say: **I'd have to say that we have a fairly complete definition of love now. But we're not finished yet!**

Ask:

• **Does anyone know what a syllogism is?**

Say: **A syllogism is a way of reasoning in which two statements are made and a logical conclusion is drawn from those two statements. For example, if I said that all mammals are warmblooded and that dogs are mammals, the logical conclusion would be that dogs are warmblooded, right? Let's see how we can use that kind of reasoning with our definition of love.**

Have groups look up and read aloud 1 John 4:16b. Then point to the newsprint.

Say: **We've already thoroughly defined love, haven't we? We've** said that love is patient and forgiving and kind and truthful and trusting and...well, I could go on and on! And according to the Bible, God *is* love. So, logically, if love is all those things we mentioned and God *is* love, then God must have all those qualities of love we defined.

Have teenagers stand in front of the newsprint and take turns reading the words on the hearts. But tell teenagers to preface each word with "God is..."

Then say: **Because God is love, he possesses all the qualities we've just named. And that's just the beginning! Everything we know about God barely scratches the surface of how huge and wonderful his love really is!**

Close with a group prayer, thanking God for his amazing love. Then let teenagers take home some of the hearts to remind them how much God loves them.

Final Stations

Topic: Jesus' Death

Supplies: You'll need Bibles, one copy of the "Five Stations" handout (p. 28), a CD of soft worship music, a CD player, newsprint or a dry-erase board, a marker, and Bible concordances (optional).

Devotion

Before the devotion, set up five stations in the room where students can have some privacy as they read the passage associated with each station. Place a Bible and a station card from the "Five Stations" handout at each station.

Have students form pairs and share how they would complete the phrase "Jesus' death means..." When partners have shared with each other, have each pair discuss their responses with another pair. When groups have finished, have volunteers share their responses with the entire group.

Ask:

• **Why did Jesus die?**

Five Stations

Station 1

Jesus invested a lot of time, energy, and emotion in the disciples. Even with the effort Jesus put forth, they still denied him.

Read John 18:15-18, 25-27.

Station 2

Jesus loved even the people who hated him most. The soldiers were particularly harsh in their treatment of Jesus.

Read John 19:1-5.

Station 3

Jesus owned almost nothing during his time on earth. The soldiers gambled for Jesus' clothes during his crucifixion.

Read John 19:17-24.

Station 4

Jesus was accompanied at the cross by people who loved him. In that small crowd was his mother.

Read John 19:25-27.

Station 5

Jesus was buried according to the traditional burying techniques. His body was prepared for his entombment by two people who loved him.

Read John 19:38-42.

• **What were the results of his death?**

• **What effects does Jesus' death have on our lives?**

Say: **I'd like you to imagine that you're standing at the foot of the cross. Please be silent for the next few minutes while we examine together what it was like to be present at the death of Jesus.**

Have students form groups of two or three. Instruct groups to travel to each station and silently follow the directions at each station. As students begin moving through the stations, play soft worship music. When students have finished, ask them to quietly discuss the following questions in their groups (write the questions on newsprint or a dry-erase board, and display them where everyone can see them):

• **What do you think was the hardest thing for Jesus to do as he was dying?**

• **What emotions do you think Jesus felt as he was crucified?**

Read 1 Thessalonians 5:9-10.

Ask:

• **According to this passage, why did Jesus die?**

• **What did Jesus' death accomplish for us?**

• **What might have happened if Jesus hadn't died?**

Say: **Jesus was killed for us. He went through anguish, severe pain, separation from God, and death so we could experience God's forgiveness for our sins. I'd like you to look into God's Word for some of the results of Jesus' death.**

Give each group a few of the following passages: Romans 5:6-8; Romans 6:3-10; 2 Corinthians 5:14-15; 2 Corinthians 8:9; Galatians 2:20; and Hebrews 9:12-28. If students are interested, give them Bible concordances, and allow groups time to look up additional Bible passages. When groups have finished, ask them to share some of their thoughts about the results of Jesus' death based on what they read in the Bible passages.

When each group has presented, have students gather in a circle. Ask students to spend time praying and thanking Jesus for coming to earth and dying for them.

Willing Sacrifice

Topic: Jesus' Death

Supplies: You'll need newsprint, markers, tape, Bibles, sticky notes, construction paper, and pens or pencils.

Devotion

Before this devotion, draw the outline of a cross on a large sheet of newsprint. Post the newsprint on a wall in your meeting area.

Have teenagers form groups of four. Give each group a Bible, sticky notes, markers, construction paper, and pens or pencils.

Say: **We know that when Jesus died on the cross, he died for the sins of the world. But what does that really mean?**

Instruct teenagers to think of any sins they've committed in the past week. Then have teenagers write their sins on the sticky notes, one sin per note. Tell teenagers to condense their sins into short descriptions such as lying, cheating, or fighting with siblings. (Tell teenagers that they don't have to identify themselves by signing the notes.) Encourage teenagers to be honest and include the "silent sins" such as having mean thoughts about someone or not following through on a kind impulse.

When teenagers have finished writing, invite them to stick their notes inside the cross hanging on the wall. Then have groups sit on the floor and face the cross.

Say: **Look at all those sins. That's why Jesus died, because we'd be buried in sin, overcome by sin, and never able to see how much God loves us. But Jesus—who never committed even *one* sin—was willing to face death alone to open the door to heaven for us. He was willing to take on the sins of the world, including the sins we just placed on the cross, so we could have eternal life with him.**

Have teenagers discuss the following questions in their groups. After each question, ask groups to share their insights with everyone else.

Ask:

• Since Jesus is God, do you think the crucifixion really hurt him? Why or why not?

• Since Jesus is God, do you think he *had* to go to the cross? Explain.

Say: **Jesus is God, but he was a man, too. Being whipped and beaten hurt Jesus just as much as it would hurt you. Having nails hammered through his hands and feet hurt Jesus just as much as it would hurt you. Being separated from his Father, whom he loved, hurt Jesus just as much as it would hurt you to be separated from someone you love.**

And, yes, Jesus could have refused to go to the cross, or he could have called angels to help him. But if he hadn't gone through with it, we wouldn't have a way to heaven. Jesus made a conscious decision to endure that agony for our sake. Listen to what the Bible says about Jesus' decision.

Have teenagers read Philippians 2:6-8, then have them discuss the following questions:

• **Do you see evidence in this passage that Jesus *chose* to go to the cross? Explain.**

• **Why do you think being nailed to a cross is significant?**

Say: **In verse 7, the Bible says that Jesus *made* himself a servant—it was a choice he made himself. And he didn't cut corners either. Being crucified on a cross was the most humiliating way to die in the ancient world; it was a punishment for criminals. But Jesus was willing to do even that so we could have life.**

And I'll tell you the most amazing part. If you were the only person on earth, Jesus would have gone through all that pain and humiliation just for you. It was a personal sacrifice for you and for me and for each person ever born. That cross where Jesus died had your name on it.

Have each person write his or her name on a sheet of construction paper. Then have teenagers tape their sheets to the cross, covering the sins. Saying each student's name, close with a prayer, thanking Jesus for his sacrifice for each person in the group.

Rolling Stone News

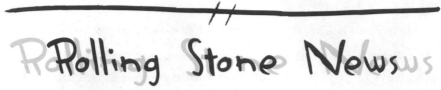

Topic: Jesus' Resurrection

Supplies: You'll need Bibles, paper, pens or pencils, and a video camera and videotape (optional).

Devotion

When teenagers arrive, ask them to be seated in a circle. Say: **I want everyone to think about a time someone important to you passed away.**

Ask:

• **What was your first reaction when you heard about the person's death?**

• **If you went to the funeral, how did it make you feel?**

• **Months later, how did you feel about the person's death? Why?**

• **What kinds of emotions do we go through as we mourn the loss of a person?**

Say: **Today we're going to talk about the death of Jesus.**

Ask:

• **How do you think the disciples felt about Jesus while he was alive?**

• **What about his mother? How do you think she felt about Jesus while he was alive?**

• **When Jesus was crucified, how do you think Jesus' family and friends felt?**

Say: **Jesus' closest friends were really discouraged and upset when he was crucified. They thought he would be around forever, and his**

death made them question everything he had told them. But thank-fully the story of Jesus doesn't end there! Ask three volunteers to read Luke 24:1-12, 13-32, and 33-48 aloud to the group.

Ask:

• **When the women arrived at the tomb, what did they find?**

• **When they entered the tomb and found his body gone, how do you think they felt? How would you have felt?**

• **How do you think the women felt when the angel talked to them?**

• **Do you think Jesus' followers had believed that Jesus really would rise again on the third day? Why or why not?**

Distribute paper and pens or pencils, and tell teenagers they're going to write and perform a newscast called "Rolling Stone News." Have them form groups of two or three, and assign each of the groups a character such as Mary Magdalene, Mary the mother of Jesus, Peter, Cleopas, or any of the eleven disciples. Ask each group to decide who will be the character and who will be the news anchors, then have the news anchors create an interview for their group's character.

Say: **Your character will be one of the people interviewed in the newscast. Focus your interview on telling the story of Jesus' resurrection from the perspective of the person you've been assigned.**

33

Ask a student to help you demonstrate an interview by reading this script together.

Say: **Here are some example questions and answers for Peter:**

Q: **How were you feeling about the death of Jesus before you talked with the women?**

A: I was very upset. I felt as if I had lost my best friend, and I wasn't sure how I was going to make it through the day without him.

Q: **What did you think about what Mary and the other women told you?**

A: I was very skeptical. I had to see it all for myself. I knew Jesus told us he would rise on the third day, but I didn't understand that this could really happen.

Q: **And what did you think after you visited the tomb?**

A: I was really curious. I wondered whether or not the women were telling the truth. I mean, Jesus' body wasn't there. So where was his body? Maybe the women *were* telling the truth.

Thank the volunteer for participating, and say: **As you create your interview, try to really develop the character you've been assigned. Try to communicate what you think Jesus' resurrection was like for your character.**

When all the groups have finished preparing, ask each group to perform its interview. You may want to videotape the newscast.

When the newscast is over, ask:

• **What did you learn by looking at Jesus' resurrection from different perspectives?**

• **Why is Jesus' resurrection so important?**

• **How does Jesus' resurrection affect you personally?**

Say: **Jesus really did rise from the dead after he was crucified. He's still alive today! He overcame death, and he gives us life.**

Close in prayer, thanking God for raising Jesus from the dead and for giving new life. (If you videotaped the newscast, let teenagers watch it before they leave.)

Jesus Lives

Topic: Jesus' Resurrection

Supplies: You'll need art supplies such as newsprint, construction paper, crayons, markers, scissors, tape, chenille wires, and clay; Bibles; and paper.

Devotion

Have teenagers form groups of three to five. Instruct each group to use the art supplies to create a series of sculptures of a caterpillar turning into a butterfly. Tell students they have ten minutes to complete their sculptures. Then have each group show its creations to the rest of the group.

Have someone read aloud Romans 6:9-10.

Ask:

• **How are Jesus' life, death, and resurrection like the metamorphosis of a caterpillar?**

• **How would you compare the mobility of a caterpillar to that of a butterfly?**

• **Besides a cocoon, what other things in nature appear to be lifeless yet are full of life?**

Say: **Jesus repeatedly told his followers that he would be put to death but on the third day would rise again and return to his heavenly Father. He said he was going to prepare a place for his followers and would one day come back for us.**

Give each group paper and crayons or markers. Say: **Spend a few minutes brainstorming in your groups about what Jesus is doing right now. Be as specific as possible. Then each group should choose a scenario that seems most likely and work together to illustrate it. Don't worry about how lifelike your pictures are—you can use stick figures if you want. After a few minutes, I'll ask each group to show** its artwork to the rest of us and explain what it illustrates.

After about five minutes, ask groups to share and explain their illustrations. Then read John 8:58 aloud.

Ask:

• **What do you think Jesus meant when he said this?**

• **Do you think Jesus was homesick for heaven during his earthly ministry? Why or why not?**

Read Matthew 28:20, then ask:

• **If Jesus is in heaven with God, what did he mean when he said this?**

• **Does Jesus' resurrection affect your outlook on life and death? How?**

Say: **The Bible says that Jesus came back to life the third day after he was crucified. When he did, he overcame the power of sin and death in the world. He promised that we can become new because of our faith in him. He changes us for the better when we give him his rightful place as Lord of our lives. And even though we can only speculate about what Jesus is doing in heaven, the Bible tells us that he's enjoying fellowship with God while he prepares a place for us. Jesus has promised his followers that we'll be with him in heaven one day. Until then, he's always with us, through the presence of the Holy Spirit.**

Lighting the Path

did this //

Topic: The Bible

Supplies: You'll need a black light bulb, a lamp, white paper, tape, treats, a flashlight, paper, pens or pencils, and Bibles.

Devotion

Before this devotion, darken your meeting area so that it's completely dark when the lights are off. Place the black light bulb in the lamp, and put the lamp in a corner of the room. Place the treats near the lamp. Tape the white paper in a winding path on the floor, leading to the treats. Make sure you move all furniture and other obstacles out of the middle of the room. Then turn off the lights.

When students arrive, have them gather outside your meeting area. Let them know the room will be dark when they enter. Let them in, then say: **Follow the path on the floor, and you'll find a surprise.**

After kids stumble around for a few moments, turn on the flashlight and ask:

- **Why aren't you following the path to the surprise?**

- **How could I help you follow the path?**

With the flashlight, lead the group to the beginning of the path. Ask teenagers to be seated.

Ask:

- **Where in our world do we find places of darkness?**

- **What are some things in our world that can produce light in that darkness?**

Say: **The Bible is a source of light. The Bible says in Psalm 119:105, "Your word is a lamp to my feet and a light for my path." The world is a place of darkness, but we can use the Bible to light our way.**

Ask:

- **How can the Bible be a source of light in our dark world?**

- **How can the Bible be a source of light in our own personal lives?**

Turn off the flashlight, and turn on the lamp with the black light bulb. Say: **Now follow the path to the surprise.**

When everyone reaches the end of the path, turn on the lights, and distribute the treats.

As students eat their treats, have them form six groups, and assign each group one of the following passages to read: Psalm 119:1-24, 25-56, 57-88, 89-120, 121-152, and 153-176. Distribute paper and pens or pencils to each group, and say: **In Psalm 119, we not only learn that God's Word is a lamp and a light, but we also discover many other amazing things about God's laws! In your group, take a few minutes to read and discuss your section of this psalm. Then write down everything about the role that God's Word plays in the psalmist's life.**

Have students share what their groups discussed, then ask:

- **Why was it so much easier to follow the path the second time?**

- **How can the Bible function like the lamp in our everyday lives?**

Lead the group in a prayer of thanksgiving, asking for strength and commitment to study and learn from the Bible on a regular basis.

Jan/Feb 2002 - Kid's got bored w/ this's

ReRead the Instructions

Topic: The Bible

Supplies: You'll need masking tape, blank greeting cards, pens, Bibles, and Bible concordances (optional).

Devotion

Before the activity, set up a life-size Tick-Tack-Toe game. Use masking tape to make three rows of three squares on the floor. In a separate area, place the pens and blank greeting cards.

Have students gather around the masking tape rows. Explain that you have a game for them to play and that they will have just a couple of minutes to play. Ask for students' ideas on how to play the game. When the youth act uncertain, say things such as "Well, what do your instincts tell you?" or "What do you *feel* is the right way to play this game?"

After several students have offered some ideas on how to play the game, ask them if it would be helpful if you told them the instructions to the game. When they agree, tell them you'd simply like them to play a game of Tick-Tack-Toe. Have students form two teams: the X's and the O's. Explain that the teams will actually send students to stand on the game board to represent the X's and the O's and that the team members *not* standing on the board will decide where the X's and O's should go. Players on the board must either cross their arms above their heads to represent an X or raise their arms in the shape of a circle above their heads to represent an O.

Say: **As usual in a game of Tick-Tack-Toe, the team that gets three** consecutive X's or O's in any direction—vertical, horizontal, or diagonal—wins.

Allow the students to play the game a couple of times. Then lead the group to the area where you placed the greeting cards and pens.

Say: **I have a good work I'd like you to complete, but you'll just have to figure out what that good work is.**

Again, when students act bewildered or confused, say things such as "What does your gut tell you?" Ask students to offer ideas about what the good work might be.

After a few students have offered suggestions, again ask if it would be helpful if you just told them the instructions. When the group agrees, explain that you'd like the students to write thank you cards to the church pastor, secretary, a volunteer, or someone else you'd like your group to thank.

After everyone has completed the cards, ask:

• **What was it like trying to complete a task without instructions?**

• **How was that like making decisions in life based just on gut reaction or feelings?**

• **How do these situations compare to what it would be like to go through life with no instructions on how to live?**

• **Where can Christians find instructions for life?**

Say: **Figuring out how to play a game or complete a task based on feelings or instinct doesn't make much sense. But that's how many of us try to go through life, making decisions based on our gut reactions. There are better ways, though. One of the best places Christians can find instructions on how to live life well is God's Word, the Bible.**

Distribute Bibles, and ask a volunteer to read aloud 2 Timothy 3:16-17.

Ask:

• **How is Scripture like instructions?**

• **What does it mean to you that Scripture is "God-breathed"? What does that say about the Bible?**

• **What's so important about being "thoroughly equipped"?**

40

• **How can you use Scripture for the purposes it's intended?**

Say: **As we can see in this Scripture, the Bible is not something God wrote so that it could sit on tables and collect dust. It's something for God's people to *use*. Scripture is *useful*. Let's see how we can use the Bible as it was meant to be used.**

Have teenagers form pairs. Explain that each partner will describe a problem or decision he or she is facing. Then the other partner will use Scripture to teach, rebuke, correct, or train the other partner. Be sure to explain that this activity is just an introduction to using Scripture for guidance and that true instruction is discovered by studying Scripture, not seeking quippy answers to life's difficult questions.

You may want to have concordances available to students so they can find Scripture about specific issues. You may also want to provide students with a couple of Scriptures that cover a multitude of issues, such as Romans 12:9-18; Ephesians 4:25–5:11; and Philippians 4:8. Above all, make yourself available to the pairs by circulating among them as they talk.

After a few minutes of discussion, have partners switch roles. After another few minutes, ask:

• **How does using Scripture compare with using feelings or instinct to make decisions?**

• **How might using Scripture prepare you for "every good work"?**

Say: **God wants us to live lives that are pleasing to him, that glorify him. But he didn't just leave us on our own to feel our way through. God gave us the ultimate instruction manual.**

The Cost of One Sin

Topic: Sin

Supplies: You'll need paper, pens or pencils, a deck of playing cards, and Bibles.

Devotion

Say: **Most of us probably have experienced chatting with some-one on the Internet. It can be a great way to meet and connect with people, but it can also be dangerous. One of the dangers is that your computer might contract a virus.**

Ask:

• **What's a computer virus?**

• **What can a computer virus do?**

Say: **We're going to play a game in which we pretend we're chatting on a computer. But watch out; one of you is the virus and can crash the whole system!**

Give each person a piece of paper and a pen or pencil. Have each person draw a card from the deck without letting anyone else see the card. (You need only enough cards for everyone in the group. Make sure the queen of spades is one of the cards.) Tell participants that the person who draws the queen of spades is the virus. Then ask them to form pairs.

Say: **This is how the game works: Write your partner's name on your piece of paper. Then you and your partner will ask each other two questions, similar to questions you would ask someone in a computer chat room. For example, you might ask, "What is your fa-vorite sports team?" or "What is your best subject in school?"**

The person with the queen of spades will pass the virus to the person he or she is chatting with by placing a check mark beside the partner's name and then showing the paper to that partner. Af-ter each pair has had some time to chat, switch partners, and start again by adding your new partners' name to your list and chatting. The two players with the virus will then pass the virus on to their new partners by again putting a check mark by their partners' names and showing the marks to their partners to let them know

they are infected. **We'll continue to switch partners and see how far the virus can spread. Any questions?**

Let the group play until the entire group is infected with the virus or after about fifteen minutes. Then say: **A computer virus can be a real problem. Today we're going to learn about a similar problem Joshua faced. Normally after a battle, the conquering army went into the city and took all the riches for themselves. But before Joshua and the Israelites brought down the wall of Jericho, God commanded them to dedicate all the silver, gold, bronze, and iron to him.**

Read Joshua 6:17-19 aloud. Say: **But not everyone obeyed the command.** Read Joshua 7:1 aloud.

Ask:

• **How many people broke God's command?**

• **Why do you think the Bible says, "So the Lord's anger burned against Israel"?**

Ask everyone who was infected by the computer virus to stand. Say: **Achan's sin was like our make-believe computer virus. Achan broke God's command, and yet all of Israel paid the consequence.** Ask a volunteer to read Joshua 7:3-12 aloud to the group.

Ask:

• **What happened to Israel because of Achan?**

• **How did Joshua respond to their loss?**

• **How did God answer Joshua's weeping?**

Say: **Just as one person infected many with our computer virus, one person's sin caused an entire nation's heartache. That's the way sin is.**

Have teenagers form groups of two or three. Ask groups to brainstorm for about five minutes and write down some sins that affect more than just the person doing the sinning, such as sex before marriage. Have them also list the people that the sin can affect, such as the parents and siblings of the couple involved in premarital sex, the unborn baby (if the girl gets pregnant), the youth group, and younger kids in the church. After about five minutes, call the students together, and ask each group to share its list.

Ask:

- **Does every sin affect more than just the person who commits the sin? Explain.**

- **Why do our sins affect so many people?**

Say: **One person started with a computer virus, and eventually it infected many people. Achan kept some silver and a beautiful robe, even though God had commanded him not to, and therefore Israel fell to its enemies. Every day each of us commits sins that affect others around us. Let's pray for the strength to follow God's will and therefore affect the people around us in a positive way instead.**

Ask a volunteer to lead the group in a closing prayer.

The Price Paid

Topic: Sin

Supplies: You'll need markers, sticky notes, newsmagazines, newspapers, and Bibles.

Devotion

Have students form pairs, and give each pair a marker and a bunch of sticky notes. Explain that the teenagers' job is to name a price for everything in the room. For example, they can decide that the curtains are worth five dollars while the ring someone is wearing is worth seventy-five dollars. Tell the group it has about five minutes to attach a price tag to as many different things as possible and that every item should have only one price tag on it.

After about five minutes, call the students back together. Then walk around the room together, discussing the different prices and how students arrived at each item's worth.

Afterward, say: **Everything has a price, doesn't it? Our society can attach a price to anything—and it does! You can even put a price on a life; the life insurance folks say you're worth whatever money it'll** take to bury you, pay off your debts, and leave a little for living family members. That's how life insurance companies determine what your life is worth.

Let's talk about payment for other intangible things.

Set out newsmagazines and newspapers, and have students look through them for examples of people paying for things they don't necessarily buy in stores, such as publicity or paying for crimes.

After a few minutes, ask students to share what they found. Then ask:

• **What intangible things does our society expect people to pay for?**

• **What are those things worth to our society?**

After teenagers have shared their discoveries, say: **Our society expects full payment even for things we can't touch. So how do you pay for ruining someone's reputation, for example? How do you pay for giving bad advice? How do you pay for abusing someone? Our society expects payment for those things, doesn't it? We pay fines for slander and acts of malice. We're sued if we give bad advice. We pay jail time for abuse. Our society calls this justice.**

Ask:

• **What kind of payment should justice demand for scorning our Creator?**

Say: **When we sin—when we do anything contrary to what God wants us to do—we're saying to God, "I don't care what you have to say. I'm smarter and better than you! I'm doing it *my* way!" Let's see what the Bible has to say about the payment required for justice to be done in this case.**

Read aloud Romans 6:23a, then ask:

• **What's your reaction to this pronouncement of justice?**

• **How does it feel to know that every time we do something contrary to what God desires, the payment we owe is death?**

Say: **The Bible says that God is perfectly just; God wouldn't demand payment greater than what was owed. So in a world of perfect justice, sin would indeed be met with death. But that's not the** end of the story, and that's not the end of Romans 6:23.

Ask a volunteer to read the entire verse aloud.

Say: **To illustrate this verse, let's collect all the price tags we placed around the room. As you collect each price tag, think about how the price listed on it compares with the price of your sin. According to Romans 6:23, what *is* the price of your sin? Write your answer on each of the price tags you collect.**

Give students a minute to collect the sticky notes, and have them keep the notes to use later. Ask:

• **As you look around the room now, how does what you see illustrate the gift of God described in Romans 6:23?**

• **What's your response to God's gift?**

Say: **There's one other element of this verse I'd like us to explore. You see, perfect justice demands payment for our sin, and God is perfectly just. The price couldn't just be removed or wiped out.**

Ask a volunteer to stand next to you and represent Jesus. Then have each student place the sticky notes he or she collected on the volunteer. Ask students to think about their sin as they attach each sticky note to the volunteer.

Ask:

• **According to Romans 6:23, the "gift of God is eternal life in *Christ Jesus our Lord*." What does that mean?**

• **How does our volunteer represent what Jesus did for us?**

Say: **Again, perfect justice meant there had to be payment for people's sins—even future sins like the ones you and I commit. Just as our volunteer is bearing our price tags, Jesus bore the price for our sins. We no longer have to pay the penalty of death ourselves because Jesus did it for us. For those who accept Jesus' free gift, our penalty is paid in full.**

Ask:

• **How does it feel to know that Jesus paid with his life for each of your sins?**

- **What's your response to Jesus?**

- **What's your response to God for providing a way to eternal life?**

Say: **In our world, we hardly ever get something for nothing. In God's world though, we get the best something—payment for our sins, which leads to eternal life instead of death—by making a faith commitment to Jesus.**

Frequent Forgiveness

Topic: Forgiveness

Supplies: You'll need Bibles, scissors, and a large pile of newspapers. You'll also need enough rubber bands to make a rubber band ball and enough leftover rubber bands to distribute several to each student. The rubber bands should be large enough to fit around students' wrists without cutting off circulation or causing discomfort.

Devotion

Before the devotion, use rubber bands to fashion a ball. Select two good-natured students from your group, and explain the following activity to them in advance.

When everyone has arrived, one of the volunteers will sit in front of the group and use a rubber band to bundle up a large pile of newspapers. The other volunteer should then come up to the front and use scissors to cut the rubber band so the papers become unbundled. After he or she cuts the rubber band, the student should say, "I'm sorry" and sit back down. Have the students repeat this same scenario several times, each time with a very insincere apology. After several times, ask the students to stop.

Ask:

- **Do you have a hard time forgiving people for the same mistakes again and again? Why or why not?**

• **What makes this especially hard to do?**

• **Have you ever found yourself apologizing to God again and again for the same sin?**

• **What is the difference between apology and repentance?**

• **How should God's forgiveness and patience toward us affect the way we respond to the people who hurt us?**

Read Matthew 18:15-20 aloud, emphasizing verse 20.

Ask:

• **Considering the surrounding verses, what do you think this verse means?**

Say: **This verse is frequently used in reference to corporate prayer. Jesus isn't saying that God hears and answers the prayers of groups better than he hears those of individuals. When Jesus speaks of two or three coming together, he is speaking of people being reconciled. Jesus is pleased when we make amends, and he's right there in the middle of reconciliation, blessing it.**

Continue reading verses 21-22.

Say: **Jesus isn't just saying to forgive many, many times; he's saying that we are to be above counting. Let's participate in a melodrama to illustrate this point.**

Read the following melodrama, choosing participants to silently role-play the king, the accountant, the minstrels, the jokers, Palo, Pete, and the jailers.

Say: **Once upon a time there lived a good king who listened while minstrels sang really depressing songs about cattle and jokers told puns that weren't even the least bit funny (these are still being circulated today on e-mail). Bored and annoyed, the king called his royal accountant. Being a very rich king, he went to work with his loyal accountant and began to count all the gold coins in the treasury, a fun thing to do for really rich people. They laughed and talked as they counted.**

"Say," said the accountant, "dost thou remember thy servant Palo? He borrowed fifty gold coins from thee last year to bet on the

jousting match!"

"Hey," answered the king, "he never paideth me back!"

Palo was brought at once to the king's throne.

"Thou oweth me much fundage," said the king. "What sayest thou?"

"I'll pay thee back, thy royal highness, I just need more time!" begged Palo.

"Aye, thou will pay me back. Thee and thy wife will wash my dishes for as long as it takes to repay the debt," answered the king.

"Please, sir, just giveth me a little longer," sobbed Palo.

The good king had pity on Palo. It was obvious that Palo was poor and the king had much. With compassion, the king canceled Palo's debt. Palo didn't have to pay back a single coin. The king shook Palo's hand and sent him on his way with a tasty bean dish and some sandwiches. Moved by the king's kindness, the royal accountant wiped away a tear.

On Palo's way home, he visited the home of Pete, an old acquaintance. That nasty Palo, he grabbed Pete by the neck and yelled, "Pay me back what thou owest me!"

Pete was startled and alarmed! "Dost thou mean the money for the soda last Tuesday?"

"That's right!" screamed Palo. "Pay up."

"Please be patient with me, Palo; I will pay thee back!" Pete begged.

Palo wouldn't hear of it. He actually threw poor Pete into jail.

When the king heard of this, he was furious! He summoned Palo immediately, and Palo was shaking like mad.

The king said, "Thou art a terrible guy! I forgave all that thou owed, yet thou didn't show mercy on Pete! Thou art going straight to jail!"

In his anger, the king sent Palo to prison where he had to wear one of those orange jumpsuits and the jailers tormented him by saying

really mean things and flicking bugs at him.

And Pete and the king and the accountant lived happily ever after.

Invite a student to read Matthew 18:23-35 aloud.

Ask:

• **How is God like the king in this story?**

• **How do we sometimes resemble the unforgiving servant?**

• **How can we forgive from the heart without holding a secret grudge?**

• **What steps can we take to restore damaged relationships?**

Say: **Think about people in your life you've had trouble forgiving.**

Distribute rubber bands, encouraging teenagers to take one for each person they need to forgive. Invite them to wear the rubber bands around their wrists as reminders to reconcile with those people. When they've made amends, they can add their rubber bands to the rubber band ball, which should be displayed in the meeting area for the next few weeks. It will remind everyone of all the times God has forgiven us of the same silly sins and will reinforce the importance of forgiving others.

Up in Smoke

Topic: Forgiveness

Supplies: You'll need Bibles, index cards, pens or pencils, an empty metal coffee can, and matches.

Devotion

Begin by discussing the following questions.

Ask:

• **When people come to you and admit that they have wronged you, are you honestly able to forgive them?**

- **How do you know when you've truly forgiven someone?**

- **When someone asks you for forgiveness, how easy is it for you to forget the wrong?**

- **Would you be more likely to go to someone for forgiveness if you knew they wouldn't remember your past mistakes? Why or why not?**

- **How easily can you remember when someone wronged you in the last few months? the last few years? many years ago?**

Say: **When we've forgiven a friend, it can still be very hard for us to forget what that person has done to us. Even if we're no longer angry with the person, the memory of those actions or words tends to remain. Years later, we may still feel the hurt.**

Let's consider God's response to us when we tell him we've done something wrong. Have three teenagers look up the following verses and read them aloud to the group: Psalm 130:3-4; Hebrews 8:12; and 1 John 1:9.

Ask:

- **What does God say he'll do when we admit that we've sinned?**

- **How can God completely forget about all the times we hurt or disappoint him?**

Say: **God is ready and willing to forgive all of our sins. He sent his Son, Jesus, to die on the cross for our sins. So when we admit to God what we've done wrong, he offers us more than just forgiveness. Our sins are completely wiped out of his memory.**

Give each person an index card and a pen or pencil. Have participants scatter throughout the room so they can have a few minutes alone.

Say: **Think about something for which you need to repent. Maybe you lied to your parents about why you were late. Maybe you cheated on a test. Maybe you used language you know didn't make God happy. Maybe you disrespected a teacher, or you joined in when everyone was picking on a classmate. Whatever you want God to forgive, write it on the index card.**

Give teenagers about five minutes to think and write down their sins. Then gather a Bible, the coffee can, and the matches, and ask the teenagers to quietly

51

follow you outside.

Go to an open, paved area, and gather in a circle around the coffee can. Then ask teenagers to hold their "sin slips" in their hands as they silently repent of their sins and ask God for the forgiveness he's already offered. After a few minutes, lead the group in a prayer, thanking God for paying the price for our sins and for erasing them from his memory when we repent.

Then have everyone in the group wad up his or her piece of paper and toss it into the coffee can. Light a match, and ignite the papers inside the coffee can. Silently watch as the papers begin to burn and disintegrate. Then read Psalm 130:3-4 aloud again. Say: **Just as the pieces of paper with our sins on them are disappearing forever, our sins disappear from God's memory when we repent of them.**

To end your time together, sing some choruses about forgiveness of sin.

Streets of Gold

Topic: Heaven

Supplies: You'll need newsprint, markers, crayons, and Bibles.

Devotion

Before this devotion, cover at least one wall of your meeting area with newsprint. Lay markers and crayons nearby.

When everyone has arrived, ask:

- **What do you think about when you think of heaven?**
- **What do you think heaven looks like?**
- **How do you think people will live in heaven?**

Direct the group to the newsprint on the wall. Ask teenagers to draw pictures of what they imagine heaven will be like.

Say: **The Bible tells us that heaven is a very real place, and not only is it real, but it's a very beautiful place.** Read Revelation 21:1-4 aloud.

Ask:

• **What does this passage make you think about?**

• **How does this passage make you feel?**

Say: **Think about a time you were terribly sad or you or someone you loved was in tremendous pain. Maybe you broke a bone or were in a car accident.** Encourage volunteers to tell the group about their experiences.

Ask:

• **What does the passage we just read say about all our pain and sorrow?**

Read Revelation 21:15-21 aloud.

Say: **John described heaven almost like a piece of jewelry. Let's add to our mural the different ways John described heaven's beauty.**

Give students a few minutes to draw additional items on the mural. Tell them that they can add anything they remember from the passage. If necessary, reread the passage as they draw.

Ask:

• **How well do you think we can truly understand the beauty and peace of heaven? Explain.**

• **How does thinking about heaven make you feel?**

• **How can thinking about heaven give us hope?**

Say: **God wrote these things so we would know there's a place without pain and mourning. He wrote these things so we could hope for our future by knowing that we will someday live in a much better place. Aren't we blessed that God has written in his Word a description of heaven? He has provided us with a brief glimpse of the future, and it serves to give Christians hope by knowing that there's a place with no tears, no death, and no mourning. That's what being in the presence of God will be like.**

Wouldn't Miss It for the World

Topic: Heaven

Supplies: You'll need baby pictures of several or all the members of your group, poster board, masking tape, paper, pens or pencils, and Bibles.

Devotion

Before your group meets, contact the parents of several students, and ask to borrow baby pictures of their sons or daughters. Arrange the photos on a poster board. Place a number below each photo on the board.

As students arrive, distribute paper and pens or pencils. Ask participants to try to determine the identity of each baby and to write their guesses on their papers. After several minutes, when everyone has finished, reveal the answers.

Say: **One of the most traumatic things you've experienced is something you can't even remember—your birth. You were forced out of a warm, dark, cozy world where you were surrounded by your mother's love. Suddenly you were in a strange, bright new world of uncertainty. The passage probably was stressful and uncomfortable, yet after only moments in your new environment, you learned how much better it is to live in the light. You could finally see your mother instead of only feeling her presence. You could see beauty, enjoy new experiences, and grow bigger, no longer limited by your surroundings. If you had never been born and had stayed where you were comfortable, think of all you would have missed!**

Ask:

• **What are some of your favorite things?**

• **What are some cool experiences that you're glad you didn't**

miss out on?

Say: **Each of us will face another passage that can be scary.**

Ask:

• **Why do you think most people are afraid of dying, even if they know they're going to heaven?**

• **What makes people nervous about heaven?**

• **Why do you think people would sometimes prefer to go on living on earth indefinitely?**

Say: **Work together with two or three others to brainstorm a list of reassurances that God might give in response to fears about death and heaven.**

After several minutes, ask groups to share their answers.

Have teenagers form two groups. Say: **Pretend you're real estate agents trying to sell the home you'll be assigned. Write a brief newspaper ad detailing highlights and selling points.** Assign one group heaven and the other group earth, encouraging each group to make its property as saleable as possible. When groups have finished, give each an opportunity to present its sales pitch.

Afterward, ask:

• **In what ways do you think heaven will resemble life on earth?**

• **How do you suppose it will be different from earth?**

• **Will you miss earth? Why or why not?**

• **In what ways will heaven be superior to earth?**

Say: **If we got what we often secretly wish for, to live on earth as we always have, think of all we would miss! We would never see God face to face or be able to touch him or hear his voice. We would never know him as he wants us to. We would miss out on the beauty and experiences awaiting us.**

Ask a volunteer to read Romans 8:19-25 aloud.

Say: **All creation feels the same frustrations we feel about life. Things aren't as they should be. When sin entered the world, so did** death. Jesus created a way for us to live forever in heaven, but while we're on earth, we're still limited by physical death. So we wait, looking forward to heaven and a time we'll live forever as God intended.

Heaven is worth any difficulty you might face on earth, and in the end it is worth dying for. The passage to get there might be stressful and even scary, but I wouldn't miss heaven for the world.

Close in prayer, thanking God for creating a place where we can live with him forever as his children.

Hell—According to Hollywood

Topic: Hell

Supplies: You will need Bibles; newsprint and markers or chalkboard and chalk; and assorted art supplies such as construction paper, glue, markers, scissors, and tape.

Devotion

Before the devotion, set up tables with art supplies for groups of about three students. When students arrive, have them form trios. If you have a large group, students can work in groups of four or five; if your group is small, students can work in pairs. As students arrive, invite each group to construct one picture of heaven and one picture of hell with the supplies available. Ask students to brainstorm in their groups how popular movies and television shows depict heaven and hell and to draw their pictures accordingly. Let them know that when they present their pictures, they will have the opportunity to tell which TV shows or movies gave them their ideas. When they have finished, pair groups to present their pictures and share what they represent with their small groups.

Say: **Discuss your pictures in your small groups by answering these questions.**

Ask:

- **Where do these images come from?**

- **Why did you choose these particular colors, shapes, or images to present to your group?**

After small groups have finished discussing, say: **We all have pictures in our minds of what heaven or hell may be like. And we may even wonder sometimes if we are going to heaven or hell. However, we have God's promise that all those who put their faith in Jesus Christ will go to heaven while those who reject the opportunity to believe in Jesus Christ and his teachings will be separated from God in hell.**

Have students form pairs.

Say: **What would happen if your parents caught you lying? Think of the punishment your parents could give you that would just make you miserable, such as being grounded and missing the homecoming football game or having to wash the dishes every night after dinner for a whole month. In five seconds or less, describe the punishment to your partner.**

When students have finished, read 2 Thessalonians 1:5-10.

Ask:

- **What are some pictures of hell this passage makes you think of?**

- **Are those pictures anything like the picture you just created? Why or why not?**

- **What do you think *eternal* punishment would be like? How does it compare with the punishment for lying that you just described to your partner?**

- **According to the passage, who is going to be punished and why?**

- **How does this make you feel? Why?**

Say: **This passage offers assurance to those who believe in Jesus. It also says that punishment will be severe for those who choose not to believe in Jesus or put faith in his Word.**

Ask:

• **Think about what it means to be shut out of someone's life—someone about whom you care very much. Are there any people in your life who you are shut out from right now? What is it like?**

• **What does it mean to be shut out from God? Explain.**

Say: **We will never be shut out from God when we choose to put our faith in Jesus. We will have eternal life in heaven because we *believe in God*. We won't have eternal life in heaven just because we *fear hell*. There is a big difference in those two statements!**

Have students form new groups of two to four, and have them discuss the following questions:

• **Do you think the idea of going to hell is meant to scare us into believing in God? Why or why not?**

• **What are some of the ways we can choose to believe in God joyfully and not just out of fear?**

• **What are some of the ways we can communicate that joy to others so that they can believe in Jesus Christ?**

Invite each group to share its answers to this final question with the whole group while you create a list of their answers on newsprint or the chalkboard.

Say: **People who put their faith in God will join him in heaven. We do not have to fear hell, and we can live joyfully with that knowledge. We can also take some of these ideas and put them into action so more people can know Jesus Christ and live without fear.**

End with a student-led prayer (or lead it yourself), thanking God for the promise of eternal life and for inviting us to join with him in heaven.

For extra impact, display the pictures of heaven and hell as well as the list of ways to communicate God's love where students can see them for several weeks. These will be great reminders for the students as well as an encouragement for those who come into your meeting room.

Is Hell Real?

Topic: Hell

Supplies: You'll need Bibles.

Devotion

Say: **Today we're going to talk about hell. There are many different opinions in the world concerning hell. Let's look at what God's Word tells us about it.**

Ask:

• **Do you believe hell is real? Why or why not?**

• **What do you picture when you think of hell?**

Have students open their Bibles to Luke 16:19-31. Ask one person or a few volunteers to read the passage aloud.

Ask:

• **Who are the main characters in the story?**

• **How did the rich man treat Lazarus on earth?**

• **Why is this so important to the story?**

• **What were some of the sins the rich man committed?**

Say: **Jesus was talking to the Pharisees when he was telling this story. The Pharisees loved money and power, and Jesus knew their hearts. This love of money was one of the basic sins of the rich man. His life was a constant party. He loved living it up on earth, enjoying his wealth and power, rather than loving the One who gave him life. And he proved this by having no compassion for people less fortunate than he was.**

Ask three volunteers to role-play Abraham, Lazarus, and the rich man. To involve the entire group, have everyone else role-play extras. For example, have two to four people role-play the angels in Luke 16:22. While the rich man is in hell, have a few teenagers role-play others in hell with him, experiencing the same torment. Have five people role-play the rich man's brothers, feasting and playing throughout the entire production.

Read the passage aloud again. As you read, have the actors role-play their assigned parts. You may have to give some stage directions as you read. For example, when the Bible refers to the angels carrying Lazarus to Abraham, you may have to encourage the angels to physically help Lazarus get to Abraham.

After the group has acted out the story, ask:

• **How would it feel to be the rich man at the beginning of the story? How about at the end?**

• **How would it feel to be Lazarus at the beginning of the story? How about at the end?**

• **Which person would you rather be? Why?**

Say: **The Bible teaches that hell is very real, and this passage depicts hell as a terrible place. It says that whoever ends up there will be in agony. It's really scary to think that we could spend eternity in a place of such misery. The worst agony to endure in hell is separation from God and anything that is good, forever. What a blessing that our loving God has provided a way for us to escape this awful place!**

Ask:

• **What way did God provide for us to escape the misery of hell?**

• **What do we have to do to be sure we won't be separated from God forever?**

Say: **Because of God's love, he sent his only Son, Jesus, to die for us. God can't allow sin into heaven, so Jesus paid the price for our sin. That way, if we accept his sacrifice on our behalf, we have the opportunity to spend eternal life in heaven with God.**

After this devotion, you may want to make yourself available to talk with students who want to understand more about accepting Jesus' sacrifice.

Jesus Is the Rock

Topic: The Church

Supplies: You'll need one piece of poster board or card-stock paper for each person, newspaper or dropcloths, several colors of paint, paintbrushes, tables, Bibles, old shirts or paint smocks, and a large plain banner.

Devotion

Before this devotion, prepare the room for painting by covering the tables and floors with newspaper or dropcloths. Place paintbrushes and various colors of paint on a table. Create a large banner that says, "Who Do You Say He Is?" and post it on a wall in your meeting area.

Read Matthew 16:13-19 aloud.

Say: **We're going to learn about the church today. Jesus talked about the church in this passage. He also asked the most important question you'll ever have to answer. And Peter gave the answer that Jesus said would be the foundation of his entire church.**

Ask:

• **What's the important question Jesus asked Peter and the disciples?**

• **How did Jesus reply to Peter's response?**

• **What rock was Jesus talking about when he said, "and on this rock I will build my church"?**

• **How would you respond if Jesus asked you the same question he asked Peter? Explain.**

Leader Tip

This activity provides a great opportunity for you to find out where your students stand! While teenagers are working on their posters, notice how they answer the question. If some students seem unsure of how to answer the question, use this opportunity to talk with them gently about the love of Jesus. Invite them to talk further with you about who Jesus is.

Say: **Jesus is the rock on which we need to build the church. We don't want to build it on the fun and fellowship we have at church, we don't want to build it on the committees we have at church, and we don't want to build it on the pastor of the church.**

Ask:

- **What would happen if we built the church on these things? Why?**

- **What does it mean to build the church on Jesus as its foundation?**

Say: **All of us at some point have to answer the question "Who do you say I am?" We have a choice to either reject Jesus or answer as Peter did, building our lives on the firm foundation of Jesus, the rock.**

Ask:

- **Who do *you* say Jesus is?**

- **How does your answer affect your life?**

Give each person an old shirt or a paint smock and a piece of poster board or card-stock paper. Encourage students to think of one word, picture, or symbol that represents their answers to the question "Who do you say He is?" Invite them to creatively paint their words or pictures on their posters. They do not need to explain their symbols to others—they can keep the meanings private if they'd like. Once the paint has dried, have the students post all of their pictures on the wall below the banner, creating a gigantic mosaic of symbols and words.

When teenagers have finished creating their posters, ask:

- **Why is it important to know how you answer this question?**

- **How can we build our church on the answer to this question?**

Say: **Jesus said he would build a church on the foundation of the divine revelation of who he is and the profession of faith in him. We all have to answer the question "Who do you say I am?" And on the basis of our answers, Jesus will build his church!**

Work to Do

Topic: The Church

Supplies: You'll need one photocopy of the "Model Church Pattern" (p. 64), scissors, enough cardboard to make five model churches according to the directions below, five small plastic bags, five rolls of tape, Bibles, paper, pens or pencils, newsprint, and a marker.

Devotion

Before this devotion, make one photocopy of the "Model Church Pattern." Use the pattern to cut out five sets of cardboard pieces students will use to build five cardboard model churches. Before putting each set into its own plastic bag, take one piece from each set and substitute a different piece from another set. When you've finished, you should have five incomplete sets, each of which has one duplicate piece.

Have students form five groups, and give each group a plastic bag of cardboard pieces and a roll of tape. Instruct groups to put together their churches, making sure everyone in each group is involved. (See the illustration below for

Model Church Pattern

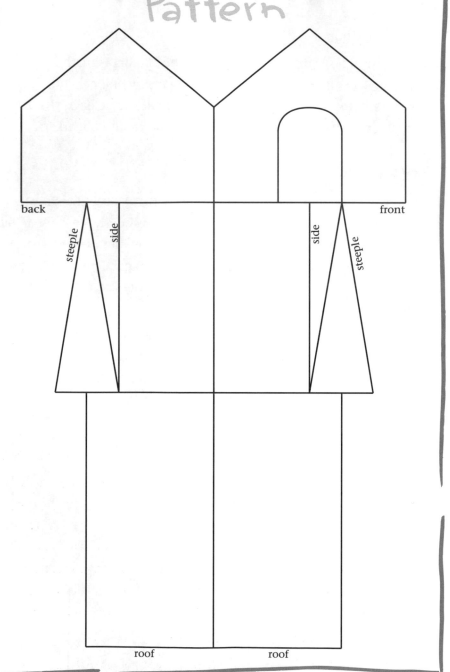

back

front

steeple

side

side

steeple

roof

roof

an idea of what the finished product will look like.) Eventually each group will realize it's missing a piece of the church.

Ask:

- **What are you trying to construct?**

- **What's the problem?**

- **Why is your group's missing piece important in the construction of a church?**

Say: **I want someone from each group to find out which group needs your group's extra piece. When you've found the right group, stay with that group and tape the final piece of its church in place.**

After all the groups have completed their churches, have someone read aloud Romans 12:4-5. Say: **Although we were only building cardboard churches in this activity, the same principle applies to the community of Christians that make up the church. Every one of us who believes in Jesus belongs to the body of Christ, and we all have work to do. Besides serving Jesus, church members are to serve one another.**

Give each group paper and a pen or pencil. Say: **Within your group, I'd like you to brainstorm the kind of work you think the church should be doing. Appoint someone in your group to make a list of your ideas.**

After five minutes, have each group exchange its list with another group. Then direct each group to identify the abilities each job requires. Finally, have each group exchange its list with yet another group. In the meantime, tape a piece of newsprint to a wall in your meeting area, and place a marker nearby.

Say: **Now I'd like you to pass the list around within your particular group. As each of you gets a turn to review the list, ask yourself whether you have any of the abilities that appear on the list. If you think you do, write your name next to those abilities. It's OK if more than one person has the same abilities. If you can't find a good match but you have an ability that isn't on the list, come up and write that ability and your name on the newsprint. Then rejoin your group.**

After about ten minutes, ask:

- **What are some things you think the church should be doing?**

• What are some of the abilities needed to do this kind of work?

• Have any of your groups listed a job but no one who is able to do the work? If so, what is that job?

Say: **If there is a group that can send someone from its "church congregation" to another to do a certain job, have that person go to the church congregation that needs someone with that ability.**

Ask:

• Is there a group that can use any of these abilities written on the newsprint? If so, raise your hands so the people with those abilities can find you.

• How large do you think a church congregation should be? Explain.

• How large does Jesus want his church to be? Explain.

• In what ways do you personally need other people in your church congregation? in the church at large?

• Besides the fact that each of us has valuable skills to contribute to the church, why are we important to God?

• How does the church differ from man-made clubs or fraternities?

Say: **Unlike many human organizations, God's church is open to anyone who wants to join. The Bible tells us that God wants everyone to enjoy his blessings and to have eternal life. What's more, we're all precious in God's eyes. He has given each of us valuable talents to use for the sake of his kingdom and for our own good. Let's each take a moment to thank God for someone else in this room and for inviting us to be members in his church.**

Encourage teenagers to think of someone in the room they're thankful for, and close with a moment of silent reflection and prayer.

Dead-Letter Office

Topic: Sharing Faith

Supplies: You'll need paper, pens or pencils, envelopes, a basket, and Bibles.

Devotion

Have teenagers sit in a circle on the floor. Give each person a sheet of paper, a pen or pencil, and an envelope.

Say: **Pretend you have the opportunity to tell someone about your faith. This person may not know anything at all about God or may be having questions or doubts. On your sheet of paper, write one important thing you've learned about God, the Bible, or your faith in general. You might write a favorite Bible verse, a truth you've learned, or a piece of advice you would give someone who is searching for God.**

Give teenagers time to think and write, then have them pass their papers to the right. Tell teenagers to write something else they could share about their faith on the papers they receive. Have teenagers continue in this manner until each person receives his or her original paper again. Then have teenagers form pairs to discuss the following questions. After each question, ask volunteers to share their answers with the rest of the group.

Ask:

• **Which statement written on your paper do you think is the most important? Why?**

• **What's the most important thing about your faith that you could share with someone else?**

• **When is it easy to talk about your faith? When is it hard?**

Have teenagers fold their papers and place them in envelopes. Tell them to think of as many people as possible they could share their faith with this

67

week and to write the names of those people on the front of the envelopes.

Say: **Sometimes we may feel uncomfortable sharing our faith. We may feel as though we'll be laughed at or ignored. But it's important to persevere because others need to know about Jesus. Tell your partner who first told you about Jesus and what kind of impact that had on your life.**

Give teenagers a few moments to talk about their experiences. Then begin to collect the envelopes. Say: **The post office has what is called a dead-letter office. It's a place where postal workers put all the letters and packages that can't be delivered.** Take the envelopes you've collected, and place them in a basket in the far corner of the room.

Say: **Think about the great news your envelopes contain. But if that news is never shared, your faith gets stuck in a kind of dead-letter office, doesn't it? People need to hear the good news you already know. In fact, Jesus tells us clearly to tell others about him. I'll show you what I mean.**

Give each pair a Bible, and have partners read Mark 16:15.

Ask:

• **Why do you think Jesus says to tell others the good news?**

• **Why is it so important to share your faith?**

Say: **Think about the people whose names you wrote on your envelope.**

Ask:

• **How might their lives turn out if you never share the information written inside the envelope?**

• **How might their lives be different if you *do* share that information?**

Have teenagers form a circle again, and pass the basket of envelopes around the circle. Let each person retrieve his or her envelope from the basket.

Say: **Don't let your faith get stuck in the dead-letter office. Take your letter home, and look often at the names on your envelope. God may want you to be just the person who tells those people about him. It's up to you to deliver that good news! Let's ask God to help us do that.**

Close with a prayer, asking God to help your students share their faith with others in the coming week.

Question and Answer

Topic: Sharing Faith

Supplies: You'll need one photocopy of the "Question and Answer" handout (p. 71), scissors, three dice, Bibles, colored pieces of construction paper, and a timer or stopwatch.

Devotion

Before this devotion, make one photocopy of the "Question and Answer" handout, and cut apart the cards. Place each set of cards in a facedown pile on a table at the front of the room, and label the three piles "Setting Apart," "Answers," and "Gentleness and Respect." Set a die in front of each pile.

Begin by asking:

- **What does it mean to share your faith with someone?**

- **What are some good ways to share your faith?**

Ask a volunteer to read 1 Peter 3:15-16 aloud, and ask:

- **What does this Scripture tell you about sharing faith?**

Say: **According to this Scripture, the act of sharing faith consists of several elements: setting apart Christ as Lord, being prepared to give answers to anyone who asks, and treating others with gentleness and respect. We're going to examine these three elements a little more closely in our very own game show!**

In your best game show–host voice, say: **I'd like to welcome you to the Question and Answer show! To begin our show, create three teams of at least four people each and name your teams.** Give teenagers a few minutes to do this. Then have each team introduce itself.

Give each team a piece of colored construction paper to use as a flag, and say: **Let me tell you the rules of the game. You'll each choose one runner. That runner will come up, roll a die, and choose a card according to the number on the die. If you roll a one or a two, take a card from the "Setting Apart" pile. If you roll a three or a four, take a card from the "Answers" pile, and if you roll a five or a six, take a card from the "Gentleness and Respect" pile. Once the runner has picked a card, he or she will run back to the team. The team will read the scenario on the card and decide a good way to handle the situation. When you think you have a good solution, hold your flag up. You'll read your scenario to the other teams, and they'll have thirty seconds to decide a solution. Then you'll share your solution with the whole group.**

Make sure everyone understands the rules, and then have each team choose a runner. When teams are ready, say: **Ready? Begin Round 1!**

When a team raises its flag, say: **Stop!** Then have the team share its scenario. Give the other teams thirty seconds to come up with solutions, then have the first team share its solution. Ask other teams to share theirs as well. Then say: **Great solutions! Ready for Round 2?**

Continue in this manner until the cards are gone. If one pile runs out before the game is over, help the runner who rolled that number think of his or her own scenario.

When the game is finished, say: **Great job! You're all winners!**

Ask:

• **What did you learn about sharing your faith with others?**

• **What's one idea from this game that you'll take with you into the coming week?**

To close, have a volunteer read 1 Peter 3:15-16 again.

Question and Answers

"Setting Apart"

A friend invites you to a party. You know there will be alcohol and possibly other illegal substances. How can you set apart Christ as Lord in this situation?

Your family has stopped going to church, complaining about being too tired on Sunday mornings. What can you do to set apart Christ as Lord in this situation?

You're surfing the Net one day, and you see a site advertised that contains some information you want, but it also contains some material that isn't appropriate to look at. How can you set apart Christ as Lord?

"Answers"

A classmate who knows you're a Christian starts bugging you, calling you a goody-two-shoes because you won't sneak out of school with him. What answer can you give him?

A friend is considering suicide and confides in you. During the course of your conversation, she asks you why you always seem so together. How will you answer her?

Some fellow youth group members are poking fun at another group member who is a little overweight and can't run as fast as the others can. They say to you, "Don't you think he could diet?" How should you answer?

"Gentleness and Respect"

Your boss belongs to another denomination, one that worships very differently than your own. One day, he begins to challenge you about the way your church worships, telling you that you might not go to heaven. How can you share your faith with him with gentleness and respect?

A group of friends is talking in the hallway at school. As you walk toward them, you overhear one of the guys in the group telling a dirty joke. He sees you and looks kind of embarrassed. How can you share your faith with gentleness and respect in this situation?

You're on the staff at a summer camp. One evening you overhear two fellow staff members sharing vicious gossip about another staff member. How can you defuse the situation with gentleness and respect?

Captive No More

Topic: Salvation

Supplies: You'll need a blindfold and a two-foot piece of rope or string for every two students, Bibles, a two-by-four (about eight feet long), a stopwatch or timer, and a dictionary.

Devotion

Before the session, lay the two-by-four in the middle of the room. Begin by having teenagers form pairs, designating one person as the rescuer and one person as the captive. Give each rescuer a blindfold and a two-foot piece of rope.

Say: **The goal of this game is to get the whole group across the plank and back ASAP! The partner with the blindfold and rope is the rescuer, and the other partner is the captive. You will really have to work with your partner to meet this challenge!**

Have them identify themselves as rescuers and captives by raising their hands, and then instruct the rescuers to blindfold the captives and to tie their hands in front of them.

Say: **Captives, listen up! You have been kidnapped by a notorious gang of evil kidnappers, which is why you are wearing a blindfold and are all tied up. Lucky for you, a rescuer has come to save you from certain death. Your only hope is to let your rescuer guide you across the narrow plank that leads to safety. Your feet must not touch the ground or you have to go to the back of the line and try crossing the plank again. Rescuers, obviously your goal is to get your partners across the plank ASAP without them touching the ground. When everyone has made it to the other side, the rescuers should take the blindfolds off the captives and then switch roles—the captives will blindfold and tie up those who were rescuers last time and take them *back* across the plank. As soon as the whole group completes the challenge, I'll stop my timer and tell you how fast you accomplished this objective.**

Invite students to begin the challenge, and verbally encourage them as they work together. When the group has finished the first round, say: **Great job! Now it's crunch time. We're going to try to beat our previous time by as much as possible. Have a group huddle right now, discuss how you did last time, and get ready for the final round.**

When students are ready, have them repeat the game, and let them know if they improved their time.

If you have more than twenty students, you may want to modify this activity by forming two or more teams. Within each team, form pairs of rescuers and captives. Make sure each team has its own two-by-four, and have all the teams complete the challenge at the same time. After the first round, let each team know its time, and challenge teams to try to improve their times during the second round.

When students have finished the challenge, have them come together, and ask:

• **What was it like to be tied up and blindfolded like a captive? What was hard about it?**

• **What was it like to be guided by your rescuer who could see where you needed to go?**

Invite a student to read John 3:16, and then say: **Do you know who the ultimate rescuer is? Jesus! The Bible tells us that we are separated from God because of our sin—that we are lost and helpless and** without hope. Yet this verse tells us that we can be rescued! By believing in Jesus, we can be saved from death, separation from God, and hopelessness, and we can find true life in him.

Have students form groups of four, and ask them to read Romans 5:6-11 in their groups. After they've read the passage, look up "save" in the dictionary, and read the definition aloud to the entire group. Say: **Webster's New World College Dictionary defines "save" as "to rescue or preserve from harm, danger, or injury." Read the passage again in your group, but replace the word "save" with "rescue."**

Once groups have read the passage, have them discuss the following questions.

• **In the game we just played, you each experienced being a captive. How is that similar to what it is like to live without faith in Jesus?**

• **What are the similarities between walking on the plank with your rescuer and living a life of faith in Jesus?**

Say: **Jesus is not just our rescuer once—he's our rescuer every day. He can rescue us from sins we struggle with, or he can bring hope in situations that frustrate us.**

Ask:

• **Has there ever been a time in your life when you felt powerless and Jesus rescued you from the situation?**

• **What is one thing in your life right now that you need to rely on Jesus to rescue you from?**

Say: **Do you have a relationship with the Rescuer, Jesus? Or are you living as a captive? If you have questions about what it means to make a faith commitment to Jesus, please come talk with me after we pray.**

Close in prayer, asking God to make the way of salvation plain to each student and help each student rely on him as the Rescuer every day.

The Key to Success

Topic: Salvation

Supplies: You'll need Bibles; a padlock with a key; and an assortment of small common household or classroom objects such as a toothpick, a drinking straw, a pencil, a paper clip, and a set of car keys. You will also need a padlock and key for each person (optional).

Devotion

Before this devotion, collect the following objects: a padlock with a key, a toothpick, a drinking straw, a pencil, a set of car keys, a paper clip, and an assortment of other small common classroom or household objects. You'll need at least as many objects as there are students in the group. Set out all the objects, except the padlock key, on a table at the front of your meeting area. Keep the padlock key concealed. The padlock should be closed.

Gather teenagers in front of the table, and hold up the padlock. Say: **I need your help opening this padlock. You'll each have a turn to see if you can open the lock with the objects on the table.**

Give each person a chance to try to open the padlock with one of the objects on the table. Teenagers may protest, but encourage them with statements such as "Keep trying; I'm sure you'll find a way" and "Maybe you're not trying hard enough."

After everyone has had a turn, have teenagers form pairs to answer the following questions. After each question, ask partners to share their answers with the rest of the group.

Ask:

• **Why couldn't you open the padlock?**

• **What would have made opening the lock easier?**

• **How was trying to open the lock without the key like how people try to find the way to heaven?**

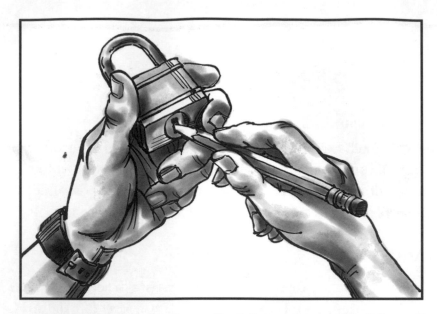

Say: **You couldn't open the padlock because you didn't have the key.** Hold up the key to the padlock. **There's only one key that will open this lock.** Use the key to open the padlock. **Heaven is a lot like this padlock. There's only one key that will open the door into heaven.**

Give each pair a Bible, and have partners read Acts 4:8-12. When everyone has finished reading, ask:

• **How would you define salvation?**

• **According to this passage, what do you think the key to heaven is?**

Say: **The Bible tells us that the only way to heaven—the key to salvation—is Jesus. There's no other way. Jesus is the only one who can save us from our sins. Without Jesus, we live our lives as if we are trying to open a lock without the right key. We can search and search and try and try, but we'll never succeed. But when we believe in Jesus, accepting his sacrifice on our behalf, the door to heaven is opened to us. Jesus is our key to salvation.**

Have teenagers join hands in a circle, and let each person say one word that expresses how he or she feels about Jesus being our key to salvation. Then close by thanking Jesus for opening the door to heaven for us. For extra impact, give each person a padlock and a key to take home.

Creative Geniuses

Topic: Creation

Supplies: You'll need the letter tiles from a Scrabble board game, four paper bags, paper, pens or pencils, a dictionary, and Bibles.

Devotion

Before this devotion, fill four paper bags with Scrabble tiles. One bag should contain the letters "HUMANBEING," the second bag should contain "PLANETEARTH," the third bag should contain "SOLARSYSTEM," and the fourth bag should contain "DESIGNER."

When students arrive, have them form four groups, and give each group paper, a pen or pencil, and one of the paper bags. Say: **Today we're going to attempt the Scrabble Double Challenge. Your groups will have only *five* minutes to complete the challenge. It's a game of chance—it doesn't really require *any* skills! Are you up for the challenge?**

Explain that all the students can do is shake their bags and dump the letters on the floor. Once the letters are on the floor, the students cannot touch them or move them around. Groups can take as long as they want to examine the letters, then they may scoop them up into the bags, shake them, and dump the letters out again. They can repeat this as many times as they'd like during the five minutes.

The first challenge is that each group needs to figure out the word or phrase the letters will spell and write it down on the piece of paper. Once a group has correctly guessed it, the second challenge is to shake and dump the bag again and again until the letters land in such a way that they form the correct order, spelling the word or phrase. Have groups keep track of the number of times they attempted to dump the letters in the correct order.

After five minutes, ask the groups to share with each other the words their letters spelled. If groups are unsure or have guessed incorrectly, give them clues until they guess correctly.

Invite the students to discuss the following questions in their group:

• **How would you describe the way the letters looked when you dumped them out?**

• **Did anything happen as you tried again and again? Or did the situation stay the same?**

• **How difficult was it to make the letters spell the words?**

• **What would have made it easier?**

Invite groups to spell the correct words with their Scrabble tiles.

Say: **Again and again the letters landed in a random way. Some landed faceup, some landed facedown, some landed in bunches, and some landed by themselves. But there doesn't seem to be any rhyme or reason to how they landed.**

Hold up the dictionary, and flip open the pages for the teenagers to see. Say: **As you can see, the words in this dictionary are all made up of the same twenty-six letters, all in different combinations.**

Ask:

• **Why didn't the letters we tossed form words each time?**

Say: **Some of you may have heard the idea that God didn't really create our universe and everything in it. You may have heard the idea that our universe was created by a chance explosion, by a physical reaction that just happened.**

Ask:

• **How do *you* think our world came to be?**

Give each person a Bible. Say: **Open your Bible to the very first verse, and read the verse aloud together.** Pause, then read Genesis 1:1 aloud as a group. **The Bible tells us that *God* created the heavens and the earth— not some chance explosion and not some natural occurrence—God! Tell your group members what you think the most amazing part of God's creation is and why you think so.**

Give teenagers a few minutes to talk. Encourage them to continue reading the first chapter of Genesis to remind them of God's amazing creativity. Then ask volunteers to share their ideas with the rest of the group.

Say: **In our activity, we saw how impossible it would be for a few tossed letters to form a few words, let alone a whole complicated dictionary!**

Ask:

• **How is the idea of a chance explosion forming our complicated universe like the idea of random letters forming all the words in the dictionary?**

• **What does this tell you about our world?**

Say: **Our world is so amazing and intricate that only our amazing God could have formed it.** Dump all the Scrabble tiles in a circle, and have everyone gather around. **Use these letters to form one word that describes how you feel about God's creative powers and the world he made.**

Give teenagers time to form their words, using the letters in the circle. Encourage everyone to share letters or even spell phonetically if there aren't enough letters to go around. Then close with a prayer, thanking God for making such a wonderful world. During the prayer, allow time for students to share the words they formed with the letters.

Discovering the Artist

Topic: Creation

Supplies: You'll need newsprint; tape; markers; paper; pens or pencils; Bibles; and rulers, chalk, construction paper, scissors, yarn, modeling clay, or any other art supplies available to you.

Devotion

Before this devotion, tape a sheet of newsprint to a wall in your meeting area. Draw five columns on the newsprint, and label the columns "actor," "musician," "writer," "artist," and "scientist." Set all the art supplies in a pile on a table or on the floor.

Have students gather around the newsprint, and ask them to call out their favorite people in each category. Write teenagers' responses in the appropriate columns. It's OK to have lots of names in some columns and few names in others. After you've written a few names in each category, ask students to spend a few moments discussing the work each person creates and why the students like it.

Then ask:

• **What is it about these people's work that makes them your favorites?**

• **What is the relationship between the artist or scientist and his or her work?**

• **What does their work tell you about them as people?**

Next tell students that they're going to become the artists. Say: **Your goal is to use the supplies to create something—a poem, a picture, a recipe, or even a mathematical formula—that says something about you. Your work should reflect something you can do, your character, or something you find beautiful. For example, someone could write a poem about a childhood memory or could plot a constellation to reflect an interest in astronomy.**

Give the students several minutes to work, and encourage thoughtfulness as they choose what to create. Circulate among teenagers as they work, offering suggestions or insight if needed.

After several minutes, have students place their creations on the floor or on a table. Give everyone several minutes to walk around and look at the creations. As students look, ask them to consider what each creation says about the person who made it.

When everyone has had a chance to view all the creations, have students sit in a circle to discuss the following questions.

Ask:

• **What do you admire about the creations you just viewed?**

• **What do the creations tell you about the people who made them?**

• **When we admire a creative piece of work, do we most admire the tools the creator used, the finished product, or the person who created such a work? Why?**

Open a Bible to Job 38, and explain that the group will share the responsibility of reading aloud Job 38:1–39:4. Say: **Each person should read about two verses and then pass the Bible on.** When everyone understands, begin by reading aloud verses 1-2. Then tell the next person in the circle to begin with verse 3, and pass the Bible to him or her. Continue around the circle until the group has read Job 39:4.

Ask:

• **What do you admire most about God's creation?**

• **What does God's creation tell you about him?**

• **When we admire something in creation, should we worship the item itself, the elements used to make the item, or God—who has the ability to create such a work? Why?**

Say: **We admire actors and artists and scientists for the work they create, and our creative works reveal something about our characters. In a similar way, God's creation reveals to us so much about his character.**

Take the group outside if the weather is nice (if not, allow the group to look out windows), and have everyone find a spot to sit quietly alone. Tell teenagers to study one piece of God's creation to learn something about what that element reveals about God.

After several minutes, have students join together again. Give each person a chance to share what element of creation he or she studied and what that element reveals about God.

Ask:

• **How can elements of creation help you know God better?**

• **What does it mean to you that God's creation is a reflection of him?**

• **How can you respond to God's creation, knowing that it's a reflection of God?**

• **How can you respond to God when you see him reflected in creation?**

Close the activity with a prayer, thanking God for revealing himself to us through his creation.

The Best Gift Ever

Topic: Grace

Supplies: You'll need four photocopies of the "John 8:1-11" handout (p. 85), a highlighter, paper, and pens or pencils.

Devotion

Before this devotion, make four photocopies of the "John 8:1-11" handout. On one copy, highlight the words of Jesus (paragraphs four, six, nine, and eleven). On the second copy, highlight the words of the Pharisees (paragraph two). On the third copy, highlight the words of the woman (paragraph seven). On the last copy, mark all remaining text to be read by the narrator (paragraphs one, three, five, eight, and ten).

Distribute paper and pens or pencils, and ask teenagers to write down their answers to the following multiple-choice questions.

Say: **Here's question one. The prize patrol is at your front door with TV cameras and a van. You've won four million dollars! You...**

a. tell them you aren't falling for that old trick!

b. tell them to come back in a week or two after you've had a chance to tidy up the place.

c. say, "Thank you very much" and "What took you so long?"

Here's question two. Your rich Aunt Bertha offers to pay your entire college tuition in memory of her departed poodle. You...

a. refuse. You could never miss the experience of paying off high-interest student loans!

b. say, "College, schmollege. Maybe if I ever get around to it."

c. thank her and decorate Fluffy's grave twice a year.

Question three: You're near death after being run over by a mean-spirited school bus driver. The doctor says your only hope is a

transplant, and he's found a donor. You...

a. refuse. You could never say goodbye to an old part of yourself!

b. shush him. *Days of Our Lives* is on!

c. accept, and thank the donor profusely.

Here's question four. While walking through the park, you notice a lottery ticket on the ground. Upon closer examination, you realize this is a winning ticket worth five hundred thousand dollars! You...

a. throw the ticket into a nearby garbage can, annoyed by the city's litter problem.

b. keep the ticket in your wallet as a good luck charm.

c. call lottery headquarters and claim your prize!

And finally, here's question five: On Christmas day, your parents buy you the stereo you've been admiring for a year. You...

a. refuse, disgusted by their careless extravagance.

b. never take it out of the box. It sits under the Christmas tree until June, when your neighbors start complaining about the tree.

c. thank them and hint about some great CDs.

Ask:

• Can you describe the sort of person who would pick mostly A's?

• Describe the sort of person who would pick mostly B's.

• What kind of person would pick C answers?

• Which of the following characters did you most easily relate to: the skeptic who felt it was too good to be true? the sick person who couldn't say goodbye to part of her old self? the procrastinator who never took the gift out of the box? Explain.

• When have you received a compliment or gift or grade or prize that you didn't deserve?

• Can you think of a time you didn't receive punishment that you *did* deserve?

Distribute the highlighted photocopies of the "John 8:1-11" handout to four students in your group. Instruct those students to read their parts dramatically aloud. Then say: **This woman was caught in the middle of her sin. Since the man wasn't also accused, it's likely that she was set up so the Pharisees could trap Jesus. The Law said she deserved to die. If Jesus told them to kill her, the crowd would doubt his compassion. If he let her go, he would contradict the Law. Jesus responded with grace. She didn't receive something she deserved—death. She did receive something she didn't deserve—a second chance.**

Ask:

• **What do you think Jesus wrote in the dirt that so drastically changed the mood of the Pharisees?**

• **Can you express what the woman might have felt as she saw her accusers walk away one by one?**

• **What did Jesus ask of her in response to his grace?**

Say: **I want you to imagine for a moment that you're this woman. You've been trapped and caught in the act of your sin. You've been brought to the feet of Jesus. You are embarrassed, helpless, and scared. Satan is there to accuse you, and you await certain death. Instead of the punishment you deserve, Christ offers you forgiveness and a second chance. Like any gift, his grace must be accepted and put to use to be of any value.**

Ask:

• **How do you feel, knowing that Christ is willing to forgive you and save you from a fate worse than death—hell, eternal separation from God?**

• **What will you do in response to his grace?**

Allow time for silent prayer, closing after several minutes.

John 8:1-11

But Jesus went to the Mount of Olives. At dawn he appeared again in the temple courts, where all the people gathered around him, and he sat down to teach them. The teachers of the law and the Pharisees brought in a woman caught in adultery. They made her stand before the group and said to Jesus,

"Teacher, this woman was caught in the act of adultery. In the Law, Moses commanded us to stone such women. Now what do you say?"

They were using this question as a trap, in order to have a basis for accusing him. But Jesus bent down and started to write on the ground with his finger. When they kept on questioning him, he straightened up and said to them,

"If any one of you is without sin, let him be the first to throw a stone at her."

Again he stooped down and wrote on the ground. At this, those who heard began to go away one at a time, the older ones first, until only Jesus was left, with the woman still standing there. Jesus straightened up and asked her,

"Woman, where are they? Has no one condemned you?"

"No one, sir," she said.

"Then neither do I condemn you," Jesus declared.

"Go now and leave your life of sin."

The Master's Card

Topic: Grace

Supplies: You'll need three index cards per person, pens or pencils, fine-tipped markers, paper, treats, scissors, a trash can, and Bibles.

Devotion

Before this devotion, write the following words or phrases on index cards, one word or phrase per card: "peace," "joy," "eternal life," "happiness," "grace," "wisdom," "good works," and "hope." You'll need one card for each person in the group.

Give each student a blank index card. Set out pens or pencils and fine-tipped markers.

Say: **Pretend that your index card is a credit card. Make up a name for your credit card, and write the name on one side of the index card. Then decorate your card with a logo, a phone number, and any other information you'd like to include. Make sure you also write and sign your name on the card.**

When teenagers have finished decorating their cards, have them form pairs. Give each pair paper and pens or pencils. Say: **With your partner, think of rules that your credit card company might require you to follow when you sign up. Write down those rules.** Give teenagers time to write their credit card companies' rules. As they are writing, display treats on a table. Then let pairs share what they wrote with the rest of the group.

After teenagers have explained the rules they wrote, say: **Now it's time to do a little shopping!** One by one, let them come forward and choose a treat. When teenagers are ready to pay for their treats, pretend to swipe each person's credit card through a scanner. Pause briefly, then tell each student that his or her credit card has been denied. Don't allow anyone to have a treat.

Have fun with this part of the devotion by hamming it up a little. You could pretend to chomp gum while you wait for the credit card approval, and you could personalize each rejection. For example, you might say, "I'm sorry, Mr. Jones, but it seems as though that last big purchase of green hair gel put you over your credit limit."

After each person has presented a credit card and been rejected, make a display of cutting each credit card in half and throwing it into the trash can. Then have teenagers form new pairs to answer the following questions. After each question, ask volunteers to share their answers with the rest of the group.

Ask:

• **What was it like to be rejected when you tried to make a purchase?**

• **How would it feel in real life to not get something you really, really wanted?**

Give each person another index card. Say: **Here's a new credit card to try. The name of the company issuing *this* credit card is The Master's Card. And the owner of this new credit card company is God. Go ahead and decorate your new card.** As teenagers are writing, put away the treats, and set out the index cards you prepared earlier.

When they're done, say: **OK, now it's time to try shopping again.**

Have teenagers approach the table one by one and try to buy one of the cards displayed there. As before, explain to teenagers that their credit has been denied.

Respond with statements such as, "Sorry, Jake, that last lie you told put you over your credit limit" or "I'm so sorry, Christa, but your last payment of three 'I'm sorrys' came just a little bit too late." This time let teenagers keep their credit cards.

After teenagers have each been denied credit, have pairs answer the following questions. After each question, encourage volunteers to share their answers with the rest of the group.

Ask:

• **How realistic do you think this game was in terms of how God treats us? Explain.**

• **How do you think this game compares with what will happen to each of us on the day God judges us?**

Say: **It's scary to think that our sins might keep us out of heaven. But that's not the way God works. Let's see what the Bible says.** Give each pair a Bible, and have teenagers read Ephesians 2:4-9.

Ask:

• **What does this passage tell us about God's grace?**

• **How would you define God's grace?**

Say: **We're all sinners, each and every one of us. If God kept track of our sins as a way to see if we deserved his grace, none of us would make it. Our sins would be too great. And the opposite is true too. If God's grace depended on the number of good works we do, none of us would make it that way either. Our good works would be too few.**

Ask:

• **So how *do* you get God's grace?**

Say: **The Bible tells us that God's grace is a gift, pure and simple. We can't be good enough to earn it, and we can't be bad enough to be denied it. All we have to do is have faith in Jesus, and God will give us his grace as a gift. Let's see what that's like.**

Have teenagers each come forward again and present their credit cards. As you did previously, pretend to swipe the credit cards, and tell the students that their credit has been denied due to their record of sin. Then pretend to swipe each student's card again, but this time say that there must have been some

mistake because his or her sin record has been cleared! Apologize for
sion, and give each person a card from the table *and* a treat.

After everyone has sat down again, say: **We *all* have a bad credit
when it comes to sin—and our sin denies us access to a great relationship with God. But just as in this game, when we develop a faith relationship with Jesus, God's grace wipes our record clean! Even though
we don't deserve it, God's grace and love for us exceed anything we
could possibly imagine. Let's thank God for his *amazing* grace.**

Have partners pray with each other, thanking God for his infinite love.

Friends With God

Topic: Prayer

Supplies: You'll need Bibles.

Devotion

Begin by forming pairs, partnering people who don't know each other very
well. Say: **For the next two minutes, find out as much as you can
about your partner. But you can't speak or write notes to your partner. At the end of two minutes, the partners who can tell me the
most facts about each other will win.**

When the game has ended, ask:

• **Did you find it difficult to learn very much about the other
person when you weren't talking to each other?**

• **What kind of relationship would you have with this person if
you were never able to communicate with him or her?**

• **How do you get to know your peers and develop friendships
with them?**

Say: **We get to know God and develop a relationship with him
when we talk with him and listen to him.**

Instruct students to stay in their pairs. Say: **For as long as you can, try to carry on a conversation in which only one partner speaks. The other must remain silent.** Time students, seeing which pair can hold a one-sided conversation longest.

When the game has ended, say: **Often our prayers are one-sided. We hand God a list of demands or just put in time.**

Ask:

• **Do you have any friends who won't let you get a word in? If so, do you feel close to them?**

• **What kind of friend do you feel close to?**

Say: **Intimacy in prayer, like friendship, comes when two people speak and two people listen. Prayer without Bible study is like a one-sided conversation. The Bible tells us God's thoughts.**

Read James 5:13-19, paying special attention to verses 16 and 17.

Ask:

• **Why do some people seem to get better results when they pray?**

Say: **It isn't so much that a righteous person has super power in prayer because of his or her goodness. Rather, a righteous person spends time in God's presence and in God's Word. Righteous people learn God's heart and will. They learn to desire God's will and pray for things that God wants. Those are prayers God can't wait to answer!**

Ask:

• **Think about your childhood. When did you ask your parents for something but they said no to keep you from harm?**

• **When have you asked God for something and later felt relieved that he didn't give you what you asked for?**

• **When has God answered a prayer in your life?**

Ask students to review James 5:13-19 and name some occasions in which we should pray. Discuss other circumstances in which prayer is necessary and appropriate.

Then encourage partners to brainstorm different ways people misunderstand or misuse prayer. For example, people repeat God's name or fancy words, talk to God only when they need things, or suppose God is there to give them all their whims and wants. Ask each pair to choose one of its ideas and develop a brief skit to illustrate how silly this sort of conversation would be between two friends. Give volunteers an opportunity to share their skits with the group.

When pairs have finished, ask:

• **What kind of relationship does God desire to have with you?**

• **What do you need to do to develop your friendship with God?**

• **What can you do differently during your prayer time to make it more meaningful to yourself and to God?**

Allow teenagers to form small groups for a time of sharing and prayer.

A Chat With God

Topic: Prayer

Supplies: You'll need one notebook for each person (optional), a spiral-bound or steno notebook, a pen or pencil, and Bibles.

Devotion

Before this devotion, set up a prayer journal by making four columns on the first few pages of a spiral-bound or steno notebook. Label the four columns like this:

Ask teenagers to form pairs. Ask them to tell their partners one thing that's going on in their lives at school. Tell them to pretend their partners are the president of the United States and to speak to their partners as they would address the president.

Have teenagers switch roles so that the "president" is now the one sharing. Then have them take turns telling each other the same thing but this time as if they're longtime friends.

Ask:

• **How were the two conversations different?**

• **Could you talk to your friend more easily than you could the president? Why or why not?**

• **Did your partner seem more or less interested and concerned about what you were saying, depending on how you spoke?**

Say: **It's important to treat God with honor and respect. We shouldn't pray as if God's a holy Santa Claus who will give us anything we want. But he does want us to talk to him about everything in our lives. We can tell him exactly how we feel, even if we don't want to tell anyone on earth.**

It's great to tell God when you're happy. And it's also OK to tell him that you're sad and hurt that your boyfriend or girlfriend broke up with you or that you're really depressed about the grade you got on your math test or that you're so angry about your curfew you're tempted to stay out late.

That's right—you can tell God when you want to do something that you know is wrong. He knows you're tempted to sin, and he wants you to tell him about it. Then you can ask him to help you resist the temptation. God wants you to honestly share your feelings with him.

Read Psalm 34:4-9 aloud.

Ask:

• **How did David, the author of this psalm, feel about telling God his deepest thoughts?**

• **What do these verses tell us about how we can pray?**

Say: **David was confident that God would hear his prayers when** he was suffering and afraid. David described the freedom that comes from honestly telling God how we feel.

One way to make it easier to talk with God about everything is to know that he listens to your prayers and answers them. Keeping a prayer journal helps you see how he does that.

Show teenagers the prayer journal you prepared earlier. Say: **Let's use this notebook to start a prayer journal for our group. We'll share prayer requests and record them in the prayer column of the journal. Then we'll form groups and pray about each request. Later on we'll record God's answers to our prayers in the journal.**

Encourage teenagers to share prayer requests, and record them in the prayer journal. Then have students form groups of three to five and pray for specific requests written in the journal.

Close the devotion by encouraging teenagers to pray for one another on an ongoing basis.

A month later, read the requests that were recorded in the prayer journal. Ask the teenagers how the prayers were answered. Record the answers in the journal, along with the date, on the same lines as the initial requests. Thank God for hearing the group's prayers as you present new prayer requests.

Use the journal each week to show how God is working in your group.

Leader Tip

God always answers prayers, but he doesn't always answer them right away! If some of your students' prayer requests have not been answered yet, share with them that God does not always answer prayers right away, and spend some time discussing what it means to be patient and to persevere in prayer.

If you choose to do so, give each person his or her own notebook to use as a prayer journal. Encourage teenagers to record their own personal prayer requests, as well as their thanks to God. Tell them to refer to the journal as they pray so they can continue to pray about unanswered requests and record the ways God does answer their prayers.

Because He Is Worthy

Topic: Worship

Supplies: You'll need paper, pens or pencils, newsprint or a dry-erase board, a marker, and Bibles.

Devotion

Distribute paper and pens or pencils. Say: **Today we're going to talk about what it means to worship God. I'd like you to pair up with someone and think of a one-sentence definition of the word "worship." Write down your definition, and after several minutes I'll ask you to share what you've written.**

Give teenagers a chance to compose and share their definitions. Have the group combine ideas to create a complete definition of worship, and write it on a sheet of newsprint or a dry-erase board so everyone can see it.

Ask:

• **Who do you admire?**

• **How do you show your admiration for them?**

• **What's the difference between admiration and worship?**

Say: **The Bible says that only God is worthy of worship and we're not to worship idols. Although we don't think of ourselves as idol worshippers, we come dangerously close to idol worship when we treasure someone or something almost as much as we treasure our relationship with God. I'd like each of you to spend a few minutes thinking about what's important to you. What competes with God for your attention?**

Once you have identified someone or something, try to find an object that could symbolize that person or thing. For example, a letter jacket could symbolize someone's love of football, or a note could symbolize a close relationship with a friend. The contents of your wallet or backpack can provide clues about what's important to you.

If necessary, you can borrow something from someone else in the room or, if all else fails, draw a picture of the symbol you're thinking of.

After several minutes, ask students to present and explain their symbols. Then ask everyone to put the symbols in a pile on the floor.

Say: **Now that you've set aside the things that can come between God and you, let's talk about why God ought to be worshipped.**

Ask:

• **What are some characteristics of God that make him worthy of praise?**

As students share their ideas, make a list of their responses on the left side of the newsprint or dry-erase board.

Then ask:

• **What has God done that makes him worthy of praise?**

As students share their ideas, make a list of their responses on the right side of the newsprint or dry-erase board.

Say: **While the Apostle John was imprisoned on the island of Patmos, he had a vision of the future in which people from all over the world were worshipping God.** Have someone read aloud Revelation 7:9-10.

Then ask:

• **How did the people worship God in the Scripture we just heard?**

• **What are some other ways of worshipping God?**

Say: **Shouting praises is one way of worshipping God, but there are many others. One author has said, "Sometimes the greatest worship is just whispering, 'Jesus,' just saying his name and letting the fragrance of his name fill your soul"** (Glory: A Jerusalem Experience by Ruth Ward Heflin). **I'd like you to form groups of three or four and share with each other what the most meaningful method of worship is for you. If you aren't sure, then share a way of worshipping that you are going to explore and try during the upcoming days and weeks.**

After a few minutes have passed, invite the students to look at the pile of symbols on the floor and to spend some time silently praying, asking God to help them refocus their lives and worship only him. Close your time in prayer by saying: **Thank you, God, for helping us open our hearts to you and express our love for you through worship. Help us to understand worship better each day as we make our relationship with you the number one treasure in our lives. In Jesus' name, amen.**

Finding Angels

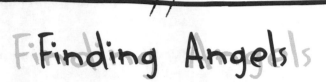

Topic: Angels

Supplies: You'll need Bibles, a CD of soft music, a CD player, four video cameras (optional), four blank videotapes (optional), and a TV and VCR (optional).

Devotion

Say: **I'd like you to look at the world around us. Let's go exploring for the next few minutes. As we walk, I'd like you to choose one thing that you find interesting.**

Lead students on a walk outside then back to your meeting room.

Ask:

• **What did you notice that was interesting?**

• **What did you notice that you hadn't seen before?**

• **What else might you have noticed if you'd had more time to look?**

Say: **Today we're going to talk about angels. I didn't hear you mention seeing them during our walk. Did any of you think about the fact that angels were all around us as we walked?**

Have students form four groups, and assign each group one of the following Scripture passages to read: Psalm 91:9-12; Daniel 8:15-19; Matthew 13:24-30, 36-43; and Acts 12:7-11.

Say: **Each of these Bible passages portrays angels acting in our world. With your group, read your passage and create a news report**

of the event as if it were happening in our world today.

If you'd like, you can give each group a video camera and a blank videotape and help the groups record their news reports as if they were in a real television studio. Encourage the students to be creative and use props and sound effects. Give groups plenty of time to create their news stories.

When students have finished rehearsing, ask each group to present its report by either acting it out or playing it on the TV.

Ask:

• **What are some of the responsibilities of angels?**

• **How does God use angels?**

Read Psalm 103:20-22 aloud.

Ask:

• **Why do you think angels praise God?**

• **What types of everyday activities do you think angels are involved in?**

Say: **Angels are all around us, and, obviously, they have a variety of responsibilities. Angels have a lot of different assignments. They're God's servants. Whatever God wants them to do, they do. They're everywhere God wants them to be. And even though you can't see them, they're working to protect you. We've learned a lot today about angels. I'd like you to take a moment to reflect on what we've talked about.**

Play soft music as students sit quietly and think about today's study. Then have students form pairs and discuss one thing they learned during the devotion. When partners have shared with each other, ask volunteers to share with the rest of the group what they learned.

The Slanderer

Topic: Satan

Supplies: You'll need two index cards for each student; pens or pencils;

a marker; three big pieces of construction paper; several pairs of scissors; tape; a dictionary; a Bible; and several tabloid newspapers such as The National Enquirer, Globe, and National Examiner.

Devotion

Before the devotion, write, "Slander Station" in big letters on one of the pieces of construction paper. At the bottom of the paper, write, "Job 1:9-11" and the dictionary definition of "slander." On the second piece of paper, write, "Misrepresentation Station," and at the bottom, write, "John 8:44b" and the definition of "misrepresent." Write, "Accusation Station" on the third piece of paper, the definition of "accuse," and "Revelation 12:10" at the bottom. Put a pile of index cards at each station. In your meeting area, set up the three stations by taping the signs in different parts of the room.

Give each person an index card and a pencil or pen, and say: **There are lots of popular movies, TV shows, and songs that depict Satan in "creative" ways. On the card that you just received, write down one movie, TV show, or song you know of that features Satan, and describe how he is portrayed.**

When students have finished writing, have each of them share what they wrote on their cards with another student. As they are sharing, put the tabloids

in the middle of the floor with several pairs of scissors. It may be a good idea to check the tabloids to be sure that they are appropriate for the teenagers in your group *before* you put them out.

In pairs, have students look through the tabloid papers and find articles that they think are particularly ridiculous or bizarre. Invite them to cut out the articles and, by visiting each of the three stations in the room and reading the definitions at each station, determine if the articles slander, misrepresent, or merely accuse a person of something.

Give students enough time to choose the best station for the article they have chosen. Then say: **Take one of the cards at your station, and write down the name of the article; a brief description of what it is about; and *how* the article slanders, misrepresents, or accuses the person featured in the article.**

When they've finished, say: **At your station, form a group, and have a member of your group look up and read the Bible passage listed on the sign at your station. When the passage has been read, answer this question: How have you been personally slandered, lied about (or to), or accused of something? Who was the one ultimately attacking you?**

Give groups five minutes to complete their discussions, then have everyone return to the center of the room. Read Luke 10:17-20 aloud.

Then ask:

• **Who is Satan? What was he originally doing in heaven?**

• **According to this passage, does Satan have power in our lives?**

• **How can we overcome him?**

• **Jesus gave his disciples authority to fight the enemy because he attacks God's people. Satan uses many strategies to do this, and three that we have looked at today are slander, misrepresentation (lying to us and about us), and accusation. What are some specific ways you can combat Satan when he comes to slander, misrepresent, or accuse you?**

Have students form pairs, and say: **Today we are going to use one of God's strategies in order to fight against our enemy—we are going to pray. Ask your partner about a specific way he or she feels that**

God may be leading him or her to fight against the enemy and what your partner is going to commit to do about it during the coming week. Next, spend some time in prayer with your partner.

The Life of a Demon
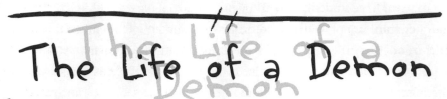

Topic: Demons

Supplies: You'll need one photocopy of the "Demon-Life Cards" handout (p. 102), scissors, newsprint, markers, Bibles, paper, and pens or pencils.

Devotion

Before this devotion, make one photocopy of the "Demon-Life Cards" handout, and cut apart the cards.

Have teenagers form pairs and sit in the center of the meeting area.

Say: **Today we're going to talk about power. With your partner, I'd like you to think of the best possible definition of power.**

Give pairs thirty seconds to create their definitions of power. When they're ready to share their definitions, give pairs newsprint and markers. Ask pairs to draw a picture of their definitions. Then ask pairs to write their definitions on the back of the newsprint.

Say: **Now I'd like you as pairs to hold up your pictures one at a time. Based on what you've drawn, the rest of us will guess your definition of power.**

Choose one pair to show its picture first. After a few students have guessed the pair's definition of power, have the pair read it to the group. Continue in this manner until all the pairs have shared their pictures.

Ask:

• **What did you learn about others' ideas of power?**

• **Is power more often seen or unseen? Explain.**

• **What effect do you think unseen powers have on us?**

Say: **God's Word gives us some very clear pictures of power. One is the power of demons. Another is God's power over demons. Let's look at these two pictures.**

Have students form five groups. (A group can be one person.) Give each group one card from the "Demon-Life Cards" handout (p. 102), Bibles, paper, and a pen or pencil. Ask each group to read the Scripture passage referenced on the card and to write its responses to the questions. When groups have finished, ask them each to get together with another group and share their answers to the questions based on their passages. If you have time, allow groups to share their responses with several groups.

Ask:

• **What did you learn about demons from this activity?**

• **Based on what you've learned so far, what kind of power do demons have?**

• **If you could draw a picture of the power of demons, what would you draw? Explain.**

Say: **You've seen that demons have some power, but now I'd like you to see the kind of power God has over them.**

Have students form two groups. Ask the first group to look up Matthew 10:1. Ask the second group to look up Luke 4:40-41. Ask both groups to read their passages and tell who has the power over the demons in their passages.

Say: **Demons have power. But God has given us authority over them. As long as we have a relationship with Jesus, God will protect us when they test our faith. Isn't it wonderful that even though demons exist, they can't do any real harm to us? And it's all because God loves us and protects us!**

Have students form groups of four. Ask groups to spend a few minutes thanking God for protecting them from demons and for giving them power over demons.

Demon-Life Cards

Matthew 8:16

- **What does this passage say about demons?**
- **What did you learn about demons from this passage?**

Matthew 17:14-18

- **What does this passage say about demons?**
- **What did you learn about demons from this passage?**

Mark 6:7

- **What does this passage say about demons?**
- **What did you learn about demons from this passage?**

James 2:19

- **What does this passage say about demons?**
- **What did you learn about demons from this passage?**

Jude 6

- **What does this passage say about demons?**
- **What did you learn about demons from this passage?**

A Servant's Heart

Topic: Servanthood

Supplies: You will need Bibles, pens or pencils, two wooden clothespins for each student, markers, photocopies of "The Servant Challenge" handout (p. 105), cups, and one pitcher of lemonade for each group of four or five students.

Devotion

Before the devotion, make sure you have enough cups and lemonade for each student and enough pitchers for each group of four or five students. As students arrive, have them form groups of four or five, and say: **You will each be served lemonade, but you cannot pour it for yourself. In your group, ask one at a time for a cup of lemonade. Each person in each group needs to ask in a different way. One person can ask politely, another can ask rudely, another could just point. Be creative, but make sure that each person is served.**

After everyone has been served, ask students to discuss the following questions in their groups.

Ask:

• Is it easy to ask for help? Why or why not?

• Would it have been easier if someone just poured for everyone and no one had to ask? Why or why not?

Say: **Every day we are faced with opportunities to serve others. Every day we are asked to put others first and ourselves second. We are called to act as servants.**

Ask a student to read John 13:1-17.

Say: **Jesus gave a very graphic example of how to serve someone. He cleaned one of the stinkiest parts of his disciples' bodies as if it were nothing. He said that we should do this for each other.**

Have students form new discussion groups of four or five and discuss the following questions.

Ask:

• Why is it sometimes hard to serve others?

• Are you ever embarrassed to serve someone else? Why or why not?

• Are you ever embarrassed to be served by someone? Why or why not?

• What are some of the messages that we receive in today's society that tell us not to serve others?

Have students form pairs, and give a copy of "The Servant Challenge" handout (p. 105) to each student. Have them complete the handouts with their partners and then return to their discussion groups to share their answers. When they have finished, ask groups to share some ways they can serve others.

Ask:

• What are some of the things God does for us that we could do for others?

• What are some very specific ways that we could incorporate servanthood into our own lives?

Give markers and two clothespins to each student. Ask students to write key words on their clothespins that will help them remember to have a servant

The Servant Challenge

The Servant Challenge

Fill in these lists, and then discuss your ideas with your partner.

List three ways that you could serve your family, such as helping a sibling with homework, doing the dishes without being asked, or helping with yard work.

1.

2.

3.

List three ways that you could serve at school, such as helping a teacher with a project, volunteering to tutor someone, or picking up all your trash and putting it in the trash can.

1.

2.

3.

List three ways that you could serve your community, such as cleaning up a park or volunteering at an animal shelter.

1.

2.

3.

attitude. Encourage them to decorate the clothespins as well. Say: **These clothespins will be visual reminders for us to have a servant's heart in our daily lives. Snap them somewhere so you will see them often, such as a folder, your locker, or somewhere in your bedroom. Put one at home and one in another place as a reminder to be a servant in more than one area of your life.**

Ask students to share with their discussion groups what they wrote on their clothespins and where they intend to put them.

End with a prayer, thanking God for the example that he set for us in Jesus, the ultimate servant, and asking God to lead students in their daily lives as they seek to serve others as he asks them to.

To Do or Not to Do

Topic: Temptation

Supplies: Bibles, copies of the "Uh-Oh!" cards (pp. 109-110), paper, pens or pencils, newsprint, and markers.

Devotion

Have students from groups of two to four, and ask:

• **What one thing would you do or try if you knew there would be absolutely no bad consequences to your actions?**

Give students a few minutes to share their answers.

Say: **Today we are going to learn about temptation. Everyone faces temptation. Even Jesus was tempted. Temptation is wanting to do something you shouldn't do or wanting something that may not be best for you. It's easy to think of things we would do if there were no consequences to them. Temptation has some very real consequences. We're going to look at a few situations that illustrate temptation.**

Give one "Uh-Oh!" card to each group. More than one group may have the same card. These cards describe a specific situation and the people involved.

There are four characters involved in each situation, two main characters and two optional characters. Have groups read their cards and assign characters.

Say: **You've all been given a tough situation. How would most people handle it? In your group, I'd like you to take just a few minutes to act out the situations the way it would happen if the characters *gave in* to the temptation they faced.**

Groups should act out their situations at the same time in different parts of the room. However, if you'd like to have an extended devotion, feel free to have each group perform its situation one at a time as the other students watch.

After the groups have acted out their situations, congratulate them on a job well done, and then ask them to act out the situations again but this time to depict a scene in which the characters *do not* give in to the temptation.

When they've finished, distribute Bibles, and ask the groups to read James 1:13-15 together and discuss the following questions.

Ask:

• **Where does temptation come from?**

• **Where does temptation lead?**

After a few minutes, say: **Our own desires can be tricky to detect sometimes. People lie or gossip because they think it will help them fit in and their real desire is to be liked. Being liked is not necessarily an *evil* desire. The real problem occurs when we desire something so much that we are willing to do anything to get it. It's when our desires get in the way of following God that they turn into sin.**

Instruct students to discuss the following questions in their groups.

Ask:

• **What temptation did the characters in your situation face?**

• **What desires might have led to that temptation?**

• **Have you ever felt tempted? When? What did you desire at the time? What did you do?**

Bring the groups together, and ask:

• **Where does the Bible tell us that temptation comes from?**

107

- **Does this surprise you? Why or why not?**

- **What desires are most common among teenagers?**

- **What temptations are a result of these desires?**

Say: **Resisting temptation can be really hard. Television, music, and news programs are full of stories of people who give in to temptation regularly. Does giving in because "everyone else is doing it" make sinning all right? No, it doesn't! So how do we resist? I'm going to read you a letter from Simon, a student facing temptation, who has written to Dear Gabby, asking for advice. This isn't a real letter, but it does illustrate a situation that many teens face.**

Read Simon's letter to the group.

Dear Gabby:

I'm not sure what to do. I'm a good student, and I play basketball on the varsity team. I go to church and volunteer with the kindergarten kids when I have time, but I have a serious problem—hey, maybe something is just wrong with me. I have lustful thoughts ALL the time...I mean, every time I see a girl I think about her in a way I shouldn't.

The ladies in my church all talk about what a great guy I am...if they only knew. My big problem is this girl Lisa. She likes me a lot—at least that's what her notes say. She would probably mess around with me if I wanted. Would giving in make all these thoughts go away? I'm having a hard time concentrating at school, and I'm afraid my grades are going to slip and I'll be suspended from the team. What should I do?

Hoping for a good answer,

Simon

Have students form pairs and write down three suggestions to help Simon resist temptation. After a few minutes, post a sheet of newsprint on the wall, and have everyone come back together and brainstorm a list of suggestions. Ask each student to identify one or two suggestions that he or she could use when facing temptation. Close with prayer, allowing some time of silence for students to pray.

Uh-Oh! Cards

Uh-Oh!

The Temptation: Cheating

The Place: A study-group meeting for the algebra final exam tomorrow

The People: A student who always gets straight A's and is super smart, a student who is struggling to get an A, a student who is doing OK in the class but is tired of studying (optional), and a student who needs to move from a C to a B in order to be eligible for a college athletic scholarship (optional)

The Situation: One of the students, the one who always gets A's on *everything*, somehow got a copy of the test, so the study group can use it to figure out all the answers before the final exam. This would help all of them get a good grade—but it could also get them suspended.

Uh-Oh!

The Temptation: Gossip

The Place: In the hallway between classes

The People: A student who works in a local store, a student who is in the "in" crowd and always seems to know what is going on with everybody, a teenage girl who comes from a large family (optional), and a student who is never serious about anything and enjoys making fun of others (optional)

The Situation: Last night the student who works in the store sold a pregnancy-test kit to the girl from the large family. The student in the "in" crowd saw it happen and decides to find out what is going on. They meet each other in the hall and begin to talk. Could the girl they saw be pregnant? This is hot news—but are their assumptions correct?

Uh-Oh!

The Temptation: Stealing

The Place: A local store

The People: A student from a wealthy family, a student who never seems to have much, a student who works part time at a pizza place (optional), and a student who seems to have everything but never works (optional)

The Situation: The students are together in the local shopping mall when they observe a lady slip a bottle of nail polish into her pocket. As she walks out the door, nothing happens—no police, no alarms, nothing. Can they get away with it too? The student from the wealthy family decides to take something. It's no big deal, right?

- -

Uh-Oh!

The Temptation: Lying

The Place: The dining room table at home

The People: A parent, a high school sophomore who got a D in math, a little brother or sister who receives mostly A's (optional), and a friend (optional)

The Situation: The high school report cards come out tomorrow, and getting good grades is really important to the parents. The sophomore student is getting a D in math, and when his or her parents find out, the student will no longer have a social life. At the table during dinner, the parent asks the student how school is going. How should he or she answer? It would be easy to avoid the conflict for at least another twenty-four hours...but is it right?

Scripture Index

Group Publishing, Inc.
Attention: Product Development
P.O. Box 481
Loveland, CO 80539
Fax: (970) 679-4370

Evaluation for *Finding the Faith Devotions* *for Youth Ministry*

Please help Group Publishing, Inc. continue to provide innovative and useful resources for ministry. Please take a moment to fill out this evaluation and mail or fax it to us. Thanks!

● ● ●

1. As a whole, this book has been (circle one)
not very helpful   very helpful

1   2   3   4   5   6   7   8   9   10

2. The best things about this book:

3. Ways this book could be improved:

4. Things I will change because of this book:

5. Other books I'd like to see Group publish in the future:

6. Would you be interested in field-testing future Group products and giving us your feedback? If so, please fill in the information below:

Name_____

Church Name _____

Denomination _____ Church Size_____

Church Address _____

City _____ State_____ ZIP _____

Church Phone _____

E-mail _____